SOul
MATTeRs

for the HEART

Wisdom & Inspiration
for the Most Important
Issues of Your Life

Copyright © 2005 by Mark Gilroy Communications, Tulsa, Oklahoma

Published by J. Countryman® a division of Thomas Nelson, Inc., Nashville, Tennessee 37214

Managing editor: Jessica Inman

For a list of acknowlegements, see page 254-255.

Unless otherwise indicated, Scripture quotations are taken from *The Holy Bible*,
New Century Version, copyright © 1987, 1988, 1991 by Word Publishing,
Dallas, Texas 75039. Used by permission.

Scriptures marked NKJV are taken from The New King James Version.
Copyright © 1979, 1980, 1982, Thomas Nelson, Inc.

Scripture quotations marked CEV are taken from the Contemporary English Version,
copyright © 1991, 1992, 1995 by the American Bible Society. Used by permission.

www.jcountryman.com
www.thomasnelson.com

Designed by Jackson Design Company LLC, Springdale, Arkansas

ISBN #1404102051

Printed in China

SOUL MATTERS

for the HEART

A Division of Thomas Nelson Publishers
Since 1798

www.thomasnelson.com

Contents

Take Care of Your Soul

What good is it if someone gains the whole world—but loses their soul?

In our mad-dash, non-stop way of life, we too often forget about—or blatantly ignore—what matters most for our lives. But deep down, the simple truth that nothing—no achievements, no pleasures, no possessions—equals the value of the human soul, resonates in our inner being. Because what we most want for ourselves is to live our lives with significance and meaning. We long to be all that God created us to be.

If you have found yourself too busy and too distracted by the hundreds of things that clamor for your attention to seek nourishment for your soul; if you have been simply going through the motions of fulfilling God's best plans for your life; if you are ready to stop floating with the currents of a joyless and shallow society in order to see a remarkable difference in your life—and profoundly impact the lives of those around you—then *Soul Matters for the Heart* is for you.

Soul Matters for the Heart tackles almost fifty of the crucial life issues you face, weaving together poignant personal reflection questions, inspirational quotes, real life stories from others, God's promises, brief—but hard-hitting—Bible studies, practical life application ideas, and prayer starters to help you to discover for yourself how to let your soul take flight and soar!

> *When you take care of your soul, all other areas of your life*
> *fall into line with God's perfect purpose and plans for you.*

User's Guide

SOUL MATTERS FOR THE HEART *is easy to follow and use, but to maximize the benefit you get from this resource, here are a few quick ideas and suggestions for your consideration.*

TO THINK ABOUT

In any area of study, when we understand how a topic relates to our specific circumstances, we experience increased levels of interest, comprehension, and retention. When you ask yourself the questions with each topic, take your time and reflect on recent events in your own life.

LESSON FOR LIFE

These quick, hard-hitting, to-the-point Bible studies are not designed to provide you with everything you need to know and "all the answers" on each of the topics, but they are designed to stimulate your own thinking and discovery learning. You will enhance what is provided here when you take the extra time to look up all the Bible passages that are referenced.

"God Will" Promises

One of the ways our souls take flight is when we truly believe in our hearts that God is good and faithful. These life-changing promises have been embraced and experienced by people of faith for centuries and have stood the test of time. When one of the promises is particularly relevant to your life, take a few extra minutes to memorize the verse so it will always be close to your heart.

REAL LIFE

True life stories are an inspiring way to see how God is at work in the life of others. Some of these stories will be exactly what you need to make some important life changes and decisions. But you don't have to relate to every single person's story to discover dynamics that will help you experience God's presence more fully in your life.

ACTION

Not every Action Step found in *Soul Matters for the Heart* will be just right for you. But don't be afraid to stretch yourself and try something you would not normally think of on your own. Or let the ideas found with each soul matter prompt you to come up with an even better way to put truth into practice.

PRAYER

Let this brief prayer starter help you express your own requests, thanksgiving, and praise to God.

TRUSTING GOD

WHETHER TIMES ARE TOUGH OR EASY, FIRM BELIEF IN A GOOD AND LOVING GOD IS THE ONLY ROAD TO VIBRANT LIVING.

Never be afraid to trust an unknown future to a known God.

CORRIE TEN BOOM

TO THINK ABOUT

- Do you have confidence that God will take care of you and provide what you need—even when life is difficult?
- When things go your way, do you acknowledge that God is the giver of all good gifts?
- Do you ever wait for hard times to come before you to turn to God for help?

LESSON FOR LIFE

God will...

Hear your prayers
Psalm 18:6

Refine you
Zechariah 13:9

Give you refuge
Isaiah 4:5-6

Eventually end your
trials
Isaiah 19:20

Daily Dependence

BIBLE STUDY PASSAGE: PSALM 40:3-5

Trust the Lord with all your heart, and don't depend on your own understanding. Remember the Lord in all you do, and he will give you success

PROVERBS 3:5-6

We rightfully teach our children—and attempt to live our own lives—by the credos of responsibility, self-control, and mature self-reliance.

And yes, being responsible is a very good thing. But when our attitude reaches the point where we trust more in ourselves than in God, twin temptations, both that lead to spiritual shipwreck, suddenly confront us.

One temptation is pride, an unhealthy arrogance that slips (or roars) into our thinking when things are going great in our lives. We become convinced that we are in control of our own world.

The second temptation, despair, works itself into our hearts when we face the inevitable difficulties and setbacks of

12

life that are outside of our control—illness, a difficult relationship, an economic downturn.

Daily trusting in God—acknowledging that He is the one
source of all good gifts and success and the only safe refuge
when life is difficult—steers us from the twin dangers of pride
and despair.

Jesus once pointed to a little child and said, "I tell you the
truth, you must change and become like little children.
Otherwise, you will never enter the kingdom of heaven. The
greatest person in the kingdom of heaven is the one who
makes himself humble like this child" (Matthew 18:3-4). A
child's humility is one of trust—it pleases God when we trust
Him as a child trusts and depends on his father.

James points out that trials test and prove our faith (James
1:1-3), but we don't have to wait for challenging moments to
begin trusting God with our entire life. The good news is that
with complete and total trust in Him, He directs our steps in the
most fulfilling paths for our lives.

But he said to me, "My grace is enough for you. When you are weak, my power is made perfect in you." So I am very happy to brag about my weaknesses. Then Christ's power can live in me.
2 Corinthians 12:9

REAL LIFE

A Feast of Faith!

STAN TOLER

My dad was a miner in a West Virginia coal mining community—Baileysville, unincorporated, population sixty! Our small white frame house was located on the side of Baileysville Mountain. We had a well that provided water and a pot-bellied coal stove to keep us warm.

When I turned eleven, we moved to Columbus, Ohio, in search of a better life. My dad, only thirty-one years old, had broken his back three times in the coal mines and was suffering from the dreaded miners' disease, "black lung." But we were happy and almost always had enough to eat—usually pinto beans, cornbread, and fried bologna for supper.

Christmas Day, 1961, is the day that changed my life forever. It had been a long, hard winter. Times were tough. Dad had been laid off from construction work, our food supply had dwindled to nothing, and we had closed off most of the house from the heat in order to cut down on bills.

On Christmas Eve, Mom sadly noted that we had no food for Christmas Day and no hope of getting any. We boys couldn't understand—Mom had always called out, "Pinto beans, cornbread, and fried bologna. Come and get it!" Now there was no food in the house.

Mom said it was time for us to accept a handout from the government, so reluctantly, Dad and us boys trudged downtown, where we stood in line with hundreds of others for hours, waiting for cheese, dried milk, flour, and dried eggs. Ugh! Finally, Dad could stand it no longer.

"We're going home. God will provide!" he said. We cried, yet we completely trusted Dad's faith in God.

That night, we popped popcorn and opened gifts ordered with Top Value trading stamps. Back then, grocery stores gave out trading stamps for purchases made. You could save the stamps for redemption of gift items from their catalog. Mom saved stamps all year long and let us pick out our Christmas presents from the catalog.

Terry got a transistor radio. (We had no money to purchase a battery!) I had ordered a miniature Brownie Kodak camera. (We couldn't afford film!) Mark got a small teddy bear. Mom had lovingly wrapped each one to be opened Christmas Eve. We were grateful to have anything!

We slept well under Grandma's handmade quilts that night. While we were fearful of the prospect of the next day without food, we were just happy to be together as a family. (Little did we know that Dad would be in heaven soon.)

On Christmas morning, we were fast asleep, when suddenly, we were startled by a loud knock and a hearty, "Merry Christmas!" greeting from people who attended our church. There they stood with gifts, clothes, and a thirty-day supply of food. (Yes, dried pinto beans, cornmeal, and a huge roll of bologna were included!) Since that day, I have always believed that God will provide, and that God is never late when we need a miracle!

ACTION STEP

READ THROUGH HEBREWS 11 IN YOUR NEW TESTAMENT, WHICH PROVIDES A LIST OF OLD TESTAMENT CHARACTERS WHO COMPLETELY TRUSTED GOD—AGAINST ALL ODDS. NOW THINK OF THE TWO OR THREE MOST DIFFICULT MOMENTS IN THE LAST FEW YEARS OF YOUR LIFE. DID YOU FACE THOSE TIMES WITH FAITH IN GOD? IF NOT, HOW WOULD FAITH HAVE MADE A POSITIVE DIFFERENCE?

PRAYER

God, I give to You every difficulty, fear, and uncertainty—along with every success and good thing—and trust You to provide the strength and grace, the perspective and poise I need to trust You in all the situations of my life.

GOD'S WORD

THE BIBLE IS THE ONE SURE GUIDE TO KNOWING THE HEART AND MIND OF GOD.

For whatever life holds for you and your family in the coming days, weave the unfailing fabric of God's Word through your heart and mind. It will hold strong, even if the rest of life unravels.

GIGI GRAHAM TCHIVIDJIAN

TO THINK ABOUT

- ☛ How often do you read the Bible?
- ☛ Do you find the Bible to be comforting and strengthening or confusing and difficult?
- ☛ Do you truly believe that God speaks to people through His Word today?

LESSON FOR LIFE

PROMISES

God will...

Protect you from sin
Psalm 119:11

Speak to your heart
1 Kings 19:12

Renew your mind
Hebrews 8:10

Call you by name
John 10:3

The Benefits of God's Word

BIBLE STUDY PASSAGE:

God's word is alive and working and is sharper than a double-edged sword.

HEBREWS 4:12a

No other book has had a greater impact on world history than the Bible. Since Gutenberg invented the printing press in 1450 in order to print God's Word for common folks, it has impacted every area of life, including education, politics and government, and even church structure. But most importantly, God's Word has helped millions experience a closer relationship with God.

Why is this book still so important and beneficial today?

• *God's Word sustains spiritual life: "A person does not live by eating only bread, but by everything God says" (Matthew 4:4). The writer of Hebrews tells us that it is spiritual sustenance (5:12-14); Paul says it is refreshing water (Ephesians 5:26); Solomon says it is medicine for our soul (Proverbs 4:22); for Job, it was his daily bread (23:12).*

- *God's Word keeps us from sin: "How can a young person live a pure life? By obeying your word" (Psalm 119:9-11). If more Christians in the world read, studied, and memorized God's Word, fewer would fall in the trap of temptation.*
- *God's Word is the final authority on truth: "All Scripture is given by God and is useful for teaching, for showing people what is wrong in their lives, for correcting faults, and for teaching how to live right" (2 Timothy 3:16-17). The historical teachings of the church are very important and helpful, but it is in the pages of the Bible that we receive doctrine, correction, training in righteousness, and even godly reproof.*
- *The Word of God is more powerful than evil: "Accept God's salvation as your helmet, and take the sword of the Spirit, which is the word of God" (Ephesians 6:17). When Jesus went into the wilderness and was tempted by Satan, He overcame evil with God's Word.*
- *God's Word makes us wise: "The teachings of the Lord are perfect; they give new strength. The rules of the Lord can be trusted; they make plain people wise" (Psalm 19:7). Through the Bible, we can test the teaching of others (2 Timothy 2:15) and know what God's will is for our lives (Romans 12:2).*

God's Word is enduring and will help see us into eternal life.

In your lives you must think and act like Christ Jesus.

Philippians 2:5

19

REAL LIFE

The Bible That Just Wouldn't Go Away

LENA HUNT MABRA

It was my first week at a Christian university and I didn't own a Bible. One of my new friends quickly discovered this and gave me an old one that she had. The cover was faded and precariously clung to a few threads, so I used an old pillow sham to give the book a new cover. Although I didn't really care for the hearts printed on the fabric, it made do.

That Bible served me for two years as I referred to it many times for classes and personal times of devotions. There were hundreds of markings as I made notes after reading a scripture—scrawled lines from sermons and devotions with my dorm. There were even yellowing tear stains splattered on the silly fabric cover from the many times I spent alone with that Bible and God.

Eventually, I decided that I wanted a more grown-up Bible. I bought a beautiful leather-bound edition and had my name embossed in gold on the cover. I was so proud to carry it around with me. I even purchased an expensive, trendy cover for it. I never did have quite the same intimacy with this Bible that I had with my old one, but it gave the impression that I wanted, and made me look like a serious Christian college student.

Cleaning up my dorm room one day, I discovered the dusty old Bible on a shelf. I didn't need it anymore—right?—so I decided to pass it along to someone else. I left it down the hall by someone's door. A few weeks later, it returned at my doorstep with a note that read, "Sorry you left your Bible. Thought you'd really need it, so I'm glad to return it to you."

I took the embarrassing Bible with its pathetic pillow case cover and left it in the Business department. Sending a small mental goodbye, I was surprised to find that I was just a bit sad. That very week, it appeared again at my door. The card stated, "You must have left this while studying. I'm sure you really need this."

I really wanted someone else to make this Bible their own. So I threw it in my duffel bag and took it with me to a friend's house in another state. I left the Bible in a restaurant and said a prayer.

Five months later, I received a package wrapped in plain brown paper with no return address. It was my Bible! The letter said, "Since you left your contact information in the front, I am happy to return this to you. I'm sure you've been needing it."

Holding the worn book again, I looked at all my notes and realized that this Bible held my journey as a Christian, a record of my spiritual development. However silly it might look, I knew that this Bible was an important element of my spiritual history.

That Bible has been in my life for eighteen years now, and I've referred to my notes many times, relishing the story of how God's Word has changed me. I'm thankful for my Bible that wouldn't go away—Someone knew I really needed it.

ACTION STEP

HOW IS YOUR RELATIONSHIP WITH GOD'S WORD? ARE YOU AS FAMILIAR WITH IT AS YOU WOULD LIKE TO BE? THINK ABOUT YOUR SPIRITUAL HISTORY—WHAT VERSES AND TRUTHS ABOUT GOD HAVE MEANT THE MOST TO YOU? MAKE A PLAN TO MEMORIZE THOSE SCRIPTURES OVER THE NEXT MONTH.

PRAYER

Lord God, thank You for not leaving us without a guide to knowing You. Please cause Your Word to root deeply in my heart.

GRATITUDE

WHEN WE EXPRESS GRATITUDE, WE AFFIRM THE HEART OF OTHERS AND BUILD OUR OWN FAITH AND JOY.

If the only prayer you said in your whole life was, "thank you," that would suffice.

MEISTER ECKHART

TO THINK ABOUT

- How do you respond when you perceive others don't appreciate what you do and who you are?
- How does the recognition and respect of others motivate you?
- Do you easily and naturally express gratitude to others?   To God?

LESSON FOR LIFE

PROMISES

God will...

Delight in your gratitude
Psalm 50:23

Give you joy through
your gratitude
Philippians 4:6-7

Increase your faith
through your gratitude
Colossians 2:7

Be glorified in gratitude
Psalm 69:30

WIIFM?

BIBLE STUDY PASSAGE: PSALM 107

*Those people honor me who bring me offerings to show
thanks. And I, God, will save those who do that.*

PSALM 50:23

When the Hebrew children were freed from slavery in
Egypt, it took them forty more years to reach the Promised
Land—a trip of 250 miles that should have taken less than a
year.

What happened?   One comedian suggested that since
Moses, a man, was leading the party, he refused to stop and ask
for directions.   But the real reason is revealed in Exodus, where
Moses declares, "You are not grumbling against Aaron and me,
because we are nothing; you are grumbling against the Lord"
(16:8).   The people began to complain almost the instant they
were free—and never stopped the entire journey.   They were
ingrates.

Sounds like the day in which we live.   The prevailing attitude is WIIFM—"What's in it for me?"   When we don't get

exactly what we want, we grumble.   We blame.   We feel a spirit of grievance.   We are unhappy with our lot in life.

The antidote, the way God wants us to live, is expressing a spirit of gratitude.

That begins with thanksgiving to God for—

- *His lovingkindness (Psalm 138:2).*
- *His mighty works (Psalm 66:8).*
- *His gift of Jesus (2 Corinthians 9:15).*

David, the king after God's heart, declared: "Let's come to him with thanksgiving. Let's sing songs to him" (Psalm 95:2).

But gratitude must also be expressed to those around us. When we show appreciation to family, friends, and even strangers, we improve their self-esteem, their sense of purpose, their confidence, their motivation to do good deeds and fully engage in life.

But not only do we bless others through our gratitude, we open our own heart to more fully receive God's love and grace for ourselves.

Now, brothers and sisters, we ask you to appreciate those who work hard among you, who lead you in the Lord and teach you.

1 Thessalonians 5:12-13

A Note of Thanks

MAX DAVIS

When the miracle happened, I was overjoyed. I couldn't believe it was actually true. I—Max Davis—finally had a university degree! To this day I don't know if it was an act of God or if the professors were just tired of seeing me.

Anyway, as a demonstration of my joy, I dropped a note of gratitude to my favorite high school teacher, Mrs. Hammonds. If it wasn't for her, I wouldn't have made it to college, much less through it. During my senior year, she went the extra mile for me and helped me understand an extremely difficult subject—a subject I needed in order to be accepted into college. Mrs. Hammonds regularly met me before class. Several times during the semester, she took time out of her schedule to work with me after school. I reminded her of her sacrifices in my note.

A few days later, to my surprise, I received a letter of response back from her—a letter that forever affected my perspective on personal relations.

She had since retired and wrote how much my note meant to her. She explained that in her thirty-something years as a teacher, she received very little gratitude. She told how she had given her life to teaching, only for most of her pupils to forget her. I'll never forget the last line of her letter. "Thanks for making one old, worn-out school teacher so happy." Read it one more time, but slowly. "Thanks for making one old, worn-out school teacher so happy." Could you hear the appreciation ringing in that statement? This woman really appreciated being appreciated. What a revelation!

Ever since then I've made it a point to try to show people gratitude for even the little things they do for me. Never in my wildest dreams, though, could I have imagined the positive returns on what have seemed my small and insignificant efforts. It's amazing how far people will go when they know they are being appreciated.

ACTION STEP

IN OUR WORLD OF CELL PHONES AND TEXT MESSAGING, THE HAND-WRITTEN LETTER IS A LOST ART. THINK OF ONE, TWO, THREE, OR MORE PEOPLE WHO HAVE SIGNIFICANTLY CONTRIBUTED TO YOUR LIFE AND WRITE OUT A HEART-FELT NOTE OF THANKSGIVING. BE SPECIFIC IN REASONS THEY POSITIVELY IMPACTED YOUR LIFE.

PRAYER

Lord, You have blessed me in so many amazing ways. Help me remember that today, and express appreciation for the people You have used to bless me.

WHEN LIFE HURTS

GOD CAN WORK IN OUR LIVES IN THE MIDST OF EVEN THE MOST DIFFICULT CIRCUMSTANCES.

*God wants us to feel that our way through life is rough and perplexing,
so that we may learn thankfully to lean on Him. Therefore He takes
steps to drive us out of self-confidence to trust in Himself, for
the secret of the godly life is to wait on the Lord.*

J.I. PACKER

TO THINK ABOUT

- ☞ Have you had to overcome trauma or illness in your life? What got you through it?
- ☞ Has a close friend or family member experienced a brokenness of body or spirit? How did you help?
- ☞ Is there any condition of brokenness too tough for God?

LESSON FOR LIFE

PROMISES

God will...

Care for your needs
Philippians 4:19

Always be ready to help
you
Psalm 46:1

Hear your prayers
Psalm 9:12

Give you strength and
joy
Nehemiah 8:10

Wounded Healers

BIBLE STUDY PASSAGE: 1 CORINTHIANS 1:26-2:4

He comforts us every time we have trouble, so when others have trouble, we can comfort them with the same comfort God gives us.

2 CORINTHIANS 1:4

All of us have witnessed instances when a friend or loved one has made bad choices—or through absolutely no choice of their own have simply been confronted with a tough set of circumstances.

The message of 2 Corinthians 1:3-6 is that there is hope for the broken. No life is filled with so much pain or in such a state of disarray that the God of all comfort cannot reach down with a healing touch. Whether you are in need of a personal touch from God in your own life or are walking beside someone else who is broken, some words of encouragement include—

- *God never forsakes us (Hebrews 13:5): Even if our brokenness is of our own making, God is still kind and merciful, and always on our side. He is present in the midst of all circumstances.*

- *God can turn tragedy into triumph (Psalm 30:11): Even in the darkest moments of the soul, God provides a supernatural comfort and perspective that allows individuals to experience and exhibit God's love and power.   Martyrs have died with joy. The terminally ill have led others to experience God's love.*
- *God sends helpers (Galatians 6:10): Even though God is all-powerful and can intervene directly in healing, more often He sends human helpers, including doctors, to work on His behalf. It is no lack of faith to turn to others for help.*
- *God heals all infirmities in eternity (1 Corinthians 15:42-43): Yes, God miraculously heals people today—but not in all cases. Paul gives the eternal perspective when he reminds us: "The sufferings we have now are nothing compared to the great glory that will be shown to us" (Romans 8:18).   One day we will all exchange imperfect bodies for immortal bodies (Philippians 3:21).   Heaven is a place where there are no more tears (Revelation 21:4).*

But even the darkness is not dark to you. The night is as light as the day; darkness and light are the same to you.
Psalm 139:12

No human words or thoughts can explain away or provide comfort for certain kinds of suffering and pain.   Maybe God doesn't want us to be able to do so.   But His ultimate expression of comfort is the gift of salvation and eternal life through the death of His Son Jesus Christ (1 Peter 3:18).

REAL LIFE

Poinsettias in Bloom

NANETTE THORSEN-SNIPES

Christmas brought me to my knees as I came to grips with my recent divorce.

The year before, during a terror-filled weekend, my husband threatened my life. My two young boys and I fled, leaving behind my marriage of eleven years, my house, my friends, even my dog.

Though I had turned away from God for a season, I knew the Lord and prayed for our safety as we tried to reorder our chaotic lives.

The country was at the beginning of a recession and full-time jobs were at a premium, so I settled for a part-time secretarial position on the other side of town. By the time Christmas rolled around, I was down to my last few dollars.

David, at seven, understood our predicament, but four-year-old Donnie waited anxiously for Christmas Day. A friend lifted our spirits with a Christmas tree, and the boys and I decorated it in blue, red, and gold balls.

With my meager salary, I bought each child two small gifts, which I put under the tree.

Three days before Christmas, the needles dropped like snow, and we pricked our feet every time we walked near tree. Sadly, David and I took down the decorations and dragged the tree to the street.

Sparkling lights, brightly colored wreaths, and gorgeous Christmas trees adorned every apartment, while we took down the last reminders of Christ's birth. That Christmas morning, we sat cross-legged on the yellow shag carpet while the boys opened their gifts. One toy, Donnie's bubble gum machine, broke. I fought tears as David tried to fix it. Like our lives, it just couldn't be fixed.

A lone tear trailed my face and David said, "It's all right, Mama, we'll make it."

Though I'd turned my back on God for months, I cried out silently, *Help us, Lord.*

Later, a co-worker who'd noticed how low I'd sunk earlier that week brought an orange-colored tabby to our house. The first thing I did was put him in Donnie's lap. His eyes brightened and a smile curved upwards. Within minutes, he leaned down and listened intently to the cat's stomach.

"Mama," he said, "my kitty swallowed a motorcycle."

I did something that day that I hadn't done in months. I laughed out loud. The sound of my children's laughter exploded like poinsettias in bloom. The joy in our hearts renewed my faith.

I learned something that day. While everyone about me had a Christmas tree adorned in beauty, ours lay in a heap at the curbside. Like the Christmas tree, I was dead in my rebelliousness—until I cried out to God for help. Though not born into poverty, I tasted it, and the Lord taught me to trust Him through His mercy and His provision. God had answered my prayer for help, and I knew my little family would make it.

ACTION STEP

HAVE YOU EVER HAD A CLOSE FRIEND WHO FACED A TOUGH SITUATION? HOW WOULD YOU ENCOURAGE HIM OR HER? WRITE IN YOUR OWN WORDS A LETTER OF ENCOURAGEMENT TO SOMEONE YOU KNOW WHO IS FACING A TOUGH TIME.

PRAYER

Father, thank You for healing us and redeeming us. Thank You for strength in the midst of difficulty. Help me cling to your love and power today. Amen.

FREEDOM FROM FEAR

THE ANTIDOTE TO A SUFFOCATING, STIFLING, STAGNATING FEAR IS SIMPLE FAITH.

If the Lord be with us, we have no cause of fear.
His eye is upon us, His arm over us, His ear open to our prayer,
His grace sufficient, His promise unchangeable.

JOHN NEWTON

 To Think About

- What is the difference between healthy concern and unhealthy fear?
- Have there been times that fear has robbed you of opportunities to grow and experience special things?
- Does fear dominate any areas of your life right now? What can you do about it?

Lesson for Life

PROMISES

God will...

Help you in trouble
Psalm 46:1-2

Provide your needs and
give you peace
Philippians 4:6-7

Eliminate fear
Leviticus 26:6

Give boldness
Proverbs 28:1

Baby Steps

BIBLE STUDY PASSAGE: PHILIPPIANS 4:4-7

So He said, "Come." And when Peter had come down out
of the boat, he walked on the water to go to Jesus.

MATTHEW 14:29

Nothing can rob you of joy, confidence, optimism, and opportunities more quickly than a spirit of fear.

Behavioral scientists have long debated whether the first emotion a baby experiences is love or fear. Because of the "startle reflex," many researchers believe it is the latter.

When faced with danger, the two foundational responses that appear to be "hard-wired" into the human psyche are fight or flight. So are you a fight or a flight person?

There are many sources of fear. Some are unreasonable (to everyone else but the persons experiencing them!), and are considered unhealthy phobias. But whatever the source—a sense of the unknown, the future, physical danger, spiritual warfare, financial crises, or reputation issues—fear is real and must be faced honestly.

One of the greatest promises of God is that we don't have

to face our fears alone.   He is always with us; never will He forsake us (Hebrews 13:5).   In fact, when we truly experience His love, fear is cast away (1 John 4:18).   Why?   Love is what must be present for trust to flourish.   So remember, if you fear—

- *The past, God makes all things new (2 Corinthians 5:17).*
- *The future, God has promised you a future and a hope (Jeremiah 29:11).*
- *Enemies, God will protect and keep you (Deuteronomy 31:6).*
- *Financial problems, God will provide for your every need (Philippians 4:19).*
- *Death and dying, God has conquered the power of death and promises eternal life (Romans 8:1-2).*

Are you ready to walk boldly, with a new sense of confidence today?   Take a few steps, even if they're baby steps, toward God and let Him handle all the anxieties that trouble you.

So don't worry, because I am with you. Don't be afraid, because I am your God. I will make you strong and will help you; I will support you with my right hand that saves you.
Isaiah 41:10

REAL LIFE

Faith, Not Fear

BRENDA NIXON

We had been warned. They were discouraged and discontent, but my husband and I moved to the rural area to pastor the congregation anyway. An explosive history, resulting in an excruciating split, plagued the tiny church. Raw feelings were chafed by mounting bills for those left behind.

They dutifully participated each Sunday, but their depressed spirits made me feel lonely. I began to question: Did the congregation accept us? Would we have friends? How could we make this ministry grow? Could we pay all the bills? What if my baby needed a doctor? I inwardly criticized, *If God loves us, why doesn't He work everything out?* My fret turned to fear washing over my mind like an acid.

One morning I hastily announced to my husband, "I'm going out!" Snatching the keys, I jumped in the car, jerked out of the drive and raced through neighborhoods, farms, and roads. *I'm afraid that... What if...?* and *Why doesn't God...?* began each angry thought.

Preoccupied, I paid little attention to my route and eventually found myself on an isolated country road. There, nestled among shady trees, on the side of the road, sat a picturesque church with white steeple. I pulled the car over and gazed at this building. Curiosity got the better of me, and I climbed out and walked to the door. Tugging on its handle, I was surprised it opened.

Lining each side of the tranquil sanctuary were well-worn, wooden pews.

Reverently, I tiptoed in and glanced around. The floor creaked as I crept to a pew and gently sat. I wondered if anyone else was there, equally hushed, watching me. Time paused. I began to sense God's nearness. Not threatened by my anger, it was as if He prepared this serene respite just for me. My heart melted and accusatory remarks were replaced with, *God, help me.*

Do you love me? He asked.

Of course I did, I responded.

Perfect love casts out all fear.

My mind was guided to Psalm 112:6-7: "Good people will always be remembered. They won't be afraid of bad news; their hearts are steady because they trust the Lord."

Do you love Me? He asked again.

Yes! I responded again.

Then you should have no fear because I'm in control.

I realized the tough realities of a new ministry and multiple family concerns had replaced my faith in the Problem Solver. But God lovingly and patiently wrapped His arms around me that day, calming my fears. God was good even when things were not. With renewed faith I found my way home and enthusiastically faced my husband and the congregation. Our problems didn't instantly disappear—but my fear of them did.

Years have passed, and I've never seen that little country church again. But my encounter with a loving God that day remains fresh. I know He listens to and answers—in His own way—my slightest prayers. Of that I have no fear.

ACTION STEP

Brendan Francis says, "Many of our fears are tissue-paper-thin, and a single courageous step would carry us clear through them."

What is one fear you are living with today—and what is one step you can take to break through it? Determine a step that you can carry out within the next forty-eight hours.

PRAYER

Your love, Heavenly Father, has ever been present in my life and I will always cling to Your love with faith and trust when I feel fear and anxiety in my life. Thank You for always being close.

GOD'S POWER

WE CAN LIVE WITH CONFIDENCE BECAUSE GOD'S STRENGTH WILL PROTECT AND SUSTAIN US IN ALL CIRCUMSTANCES.

A man with God is always in the majority.

JOHN KNOX

TO THINK ABOUT

- ☞ If God is all-powerful, why does He allow bad things to happen in His world?
- ☞ How would your life change if you truly leaned on and trusted God's goodness and power?
- ☞ Have you experienced the power of God in your life?

LESSON FOR LIFE

PROMISES

God will...

Strengthen you
Psalm 145:14
Isaiah 40:29, 31

Give you victory
1 John 5:4

Give you joy and
strength
Nehemiah 8:10

Protect you
Psalm 18:35

A Paradoxical Power

BIBLE STUDY PASSAGE: 1 CORINTHIANS 1:17-31

*For this reason I am happy when I have weaknesses,
insults, hard times, sufferings, and all kinds of troubles for
Christ. Because when I am weak, then I am truly strong.*

2 CORINTHIANS 12:10

Yes, God's power is a mighty, prevailing force that cannot
be withstood by His enemies (Job 42:2). But God has most
often elected to reveal and exercise His power in the strangest
and most subtle of ways—

- *God uses "cracked pots" to minister: "We have this treasure
  from God, but we are like clay jars that hold the treasure. This
  shows that the great power is from God, not from us" (2
  Corinthians 4:7). Isn't it amazing who God can use to change
  the world? He can use people like you and me!*
- *God leads through humility: "But he gave up his place with God
  and made himself nothing. He was born to be a man and
  became like a servant" (Philippians 2:7). In God's desire to
  have a relationship of love with His people, He doesn't boss*

them around, but serves them. In emptying himself of power,
He conquered the power of death.
- God sacrifices himself: "In the same way, the Son of Man did not
come to be served. He came to serve others and to give his life
as a ransom for many people" (Mark 10:45). The earth shook
and the skies went black in the moment of Jesus' death. But
what appeared to be defeat was actually the hour of victory.
It was then that Jesus "destroyed death" (2 Timothy 1:10).
- God never forsakes us: "I will never leave you; I will never
forget you" (Hebrews 13:5). Only Jesus experienced the horrific
moment when God turned His face from His dearly beloved Son.
That allowed the rest of us to live with the confidence and
assurance that He is always present in our lives. That means
we are connected to the ultimate source of power.
- God is at work in the invisible: "God's Spirit, who is in you, is
greater than the devil, who is in the world" (1 John 4:4). No,
God does not always announce His power with a fireworks
display or other impressive signs and wonders. But where life
matters the absolute most, in the spirit realm, God has already
won and assured the victory we need to live with Him forever.

There is no danger, no enemy, no circumstance that can
equal God's power in your life.

I know that you can do
all things and that no
plan of yours can be
ruined.
Job 42:2

REAL LIFE

Gustel's Tulips

PAT BUTLER

All the problems of the inner city were outside her door. It was the worst street in the city, filled with the homeless, alcoholics, and drug addicts, a street everyone—including the police—avoided. Gustel lived on its corner. Every Tuesday evening, I walked the three blocks from my apartment to her house to share a common burden: the children of the area. How could we reach them with the gospel? With God's help, they stood a chance at breaking the cycle of addiction in their families' lives.

We talked, thought, planned, and prayed. Our conversation was lively as we discussed doctrinal and inner city issues. How was God going to miraculously change this neighborhood? Eventually we came up with a simple idea we thought would make a difference. We organized an evening of music, games, and refreshments. Musician friends offered to play, the local donut shop donated boxes of goodies, and a local church gave us the use of their community room. We distributed invitations, put up posters, prayed, and finally opened the doors. It was going to be the kickoff of a big, attractive outreach program.

We waited. And waited—till it became obvious that no one was coming. We joked in our embarrassment, "At least it wasn't for lack of planning!" Then we packed up our pride and went home. Back to the drawing board.

Spring arrived. Gustel planted tulips in a patch of dirt in the parking lot behind her apartment building, determined that the neighborhood would not only be safe, but pretty. Soon the tulip bulbs were flourishing.

The tulips had a short life. Returning home one afternoon, Gustel found all the tulip heads cut off, her garden maimed. For the first time in all the years she had lived there, her resolve broke. She called me, furious, and vowed to move out of a neighborhood so bent on destruction.

Returning outside to mourn her garden, she sensed movement—a young boy trying to escape detection. She got face to face with him and demanded, "Did you do this?"

"No, but I know who did!" he squealed. He ran to a nearby house, Gustel following like a tornado. He motioned her around back and she stormed on. On the back stoop she found her culprit, head in hands. Gustel stopped in her tracks. Nestled at her feet, in the bare earth of a backyard strewn with cigarette butts and trash, sat the tulip heads.

The boy's shyness denied any malicious intent as he rose to greet her. He gestured at the tulip heads.

"Your garden was so beautiful, I wanted one too."

Gustel looked at the tulip heads, already wilting in the dirt. Her angry tears wouldn't bring them back to life. But the little spirit wilting on the steps she could do something about. "Honey, tulips don't grow like that, but if you'll come with me, I'll show you how to make a garden."

We never needed another night of planning; our beautiful, gentle—and yes, powerful—inner city ministry was born. Beyond our plans and prayers to do something big and bold, God helped us plant seeds of life that turned dirt into gardens all over the neighborhood and miraculously opened hearts to His love.

ACTION STEP

GOD OFTEN LIKES TO BE SUBTLE. THINK BACK OVER THE PAST FIVE YEARS OF YOUR LIFE. WRITE DOWN AT LEAST FIVE WAYS THAT GOD HAS GENTLY AND SUBTLY SHOWED HIS POWER IN YOUR LIFE.

PRAYER

Father God, I need Your power in my life, and I'm grateful that You reveal Your might in such surprising and wonderful ways. Please remind me today that You are near.

BECOMING A NEW PERSON

ONE OF THE WAYS GOD REVEALS HIS POWER AND ACTIVITY IN THE WORLD IS THROUGH THE WAY HE CHANGES US.

Salvation is not something that is done for you but something that happens within you. It is not the clearing of a court record, but the transformation of a life attitude.

ALBERT W. PALMER

TO THINK ABOUT

- Do you truly believe that people can change for the better?
- Have you ever written someone off because of past mistakes?
- Have you ever been tempted to give up on yourself?

LESSON FOR LIFE

PROMISES

God will...

Give you a new heart
Ezekiel 36:26-27
Colossians 3:10

Forgive you
Ephesians 1:7

Guide your path
Proverbs 4:11-12

Do We Really Have a Choice?

BIBLE STUDY PASSAGE: LUKE 19:2-8

You have begun to live the new life, in which you are being made new and are becoming like the One who made you. This new life brings you the true knowledge of God.

COLOSSIANS 3:10

For centuries, people have debated what makes a person who they are—are we born the way we are, or do we become this way through the things that happen to us?

Some psychologists believe that everything a person does is determined by the shaping influences in their lives like parents and life experiences—some go so far as to say that once a person is five, their personality is shaped and really can't be changed.

Other people think that we are primarily a product of genetics, that our behavior and attitudes follow from the way we are "wired." Common expressions of this idea would include: "I can't help it, it's just the way I was born"; or "a leopard can't change his spots"; or "the nut doesn't fall far from the tree."

Though our genes and life experiences have a huge impact on us, aren't you glad that there is a miraculous, powerful God who is able to change even the most stubborn, damaged, sinful heart?   Paul goes so far as to say, "If anyone belongs to Christ, there is a new creation.   The old things have gone; everything is made new!" (2 Corinthians 5:17).   After a change of heart at the moment of conversion, God isn't finished with us, either. Paul says: "We all show the Lord's glory, and we are being changed to be like him" (2 Corinthians 3:18).

But you don't understand how I've been brought up.   You don't know the mistakes I've made.   You don't understand how hard it is for me to break certain negative patterns.

With grace, with faith, with the help of godly friends, you can say along with Paul: "Forgetting the past and straining toward what is ahead, I keep trying to reach the goal and get the prize for which God called me through Christ to the life above" (Philippians 3:13-14).   Because of His forgiving, life-changing power, God's ultimate concern with your life is not where you've been, but where you are going.

Though your sins are like scarlet, they can be as white as snow.   Though your sins are deep red, they can be white like wool.

Isaiah 1:18

REAL LIFE

New Heart, New Eyes

LEE WARREN

My dad ran from God for most of his life. As a young man, he attended a church pastored by a man whose actions were less than godly. After that, Dad dropped out of church, and over the years that followed met a lot of Christians whose lifestyles didn't match their beliefs. He concluded that the church was full of hypocrites and had no desire to associate with it.

After I became a Christian, he listened patiently to me as I told him how Jesus could save him from his sins. But he continually pointed to hypocrites in the church and said he didn't want to be like them. He knew he was a sinner and that he could never live a consistent lifestyle, and he refused to become just another Christian hypocrite.

Dad made his living as a photographer, often spending time on the road. On one such trip, he ended up rooming with a former pastor. The two got to talking about religion, and after the pastor listened to Dad's objections about the Christian faith, he shared a scripture that changed Dad's life: "I do not understand the things I do. I do not do what I want to do, and I do the things I hate. And if I do not want to do the hated things I do, that means I agree that the law is good. But I am not really the one who is doing these hated things; it is sin living in me that does them" (Romans 7:15-17).

When Dad returned from the trip, he asked me if I had ever read that passage. His normal cynical tone was gone—replaced with a tone of softness and sincerity. I told him I had read those verses many times and that I was always comforted to know that even the Apostle Paul struggled against his sinful nature as much as I do.

Then he told me something I honestly didn't expect: He had become a Christian after reading this passage—he finally understood that Christianity wasn't about living a perfect life, but about being saved from the sins we commit.

He then told me that just a few hours after placing his faith in Christ, he walked into a Wal-Mart and was surprised by what he saw. He said, "I didn't see short people or tall people, fat people or skinny people, young people or old people. I just saw people.

People with struggles just like me."

He asked me if such a change was normal for a new Christian. I could hardly speak without breaking down in tears of awe and joy over the change that God made in Dad's life. I took a second to compose myself, and when I could finally speak I told him that it was normal for a Christian to have compassion for people who need grace as much as we do.

Since then, God's change in my dad has been made more and more complete—his compassion has expanded, and patience and love have overtaken his personality. He still needs grace, of course—just like all of us—but more than anything, my dad is a testimony to God's power to make a heart new.

ACTION STEP

IDENTIFY A NEW ATTITUDE OR A NEW HABIT YOU WANT TO DEVELOP IN YOUR LIFE. OR, IDENTIFY AN OLD ATTITUDE OR AN OLD HABIT YOU WANT ELIMINATED FROM YOUR LIFE. COMMIT THIS CHANGE OF HEART TO GOD AND ASK HIM TO DO A SPECIAL WORK IN YOU. YOU MIGHT EXPERIENCE AN INSTANTANEOUS, MIRACULOUS CHANGE—OR YOU MIGHT EXPERIENCE A GRADUAL GROWTH AND GRACE. EITHER WAY, YOUR TASK IS NOT TO RELY ON YOUR OWN STRENGTH, BUT TO COUNT ON GOD TO WORK IN YOUR LIFE.

PRAYER

Thank You, O God, for making me a new person through Your Son Jesus. I ask You to continue and complete the good work You started in me.

GOD'S PROVISION

THERE IS NO CAUSE FOR WORRY AS GOD HAS PROMISED TO MEET ALL OUR NEEDS.

*There is but one way to tranquility of mind and happiness,
and that is to account no external things thine own,
but to commit all to God.*

EPICTETUS

TO THINK ABOUT

- 🗝 It has been argued that "worry" is a sin because it shows a lack of faith.   Do you agree?
- 🗝 What is the difference between legitimate concern and worry?
- 🗝 Do you have a rock-solid faith that God will provide for all your needs?

LESSON FOR LIFE

PROMISES

God will...

Take care of your needs
Philippians 4:19

Never leave you
Hebrews 13:5

Provide everything you
need to enjoy life
1 Timothy 6:17

Bless you as you give
Malachi 3:10

Our Generous Father

BIBLE STUDY PASSAGE: MATTHEW 6:19-34

Look at the birds in the air. They don't plant or harvest or store food in barns, but your heavenly Father feeds them. And you know that you are worth much more than the birds.

MATTHEW 6:26

For St. Paul, the issue was simple: "My God will use his wonderful riches in Christ Jesus to give you everything you need" (Philippians 4:19).

These words were not written by a man living in the lap of luxury, but rather someone who had survived shipwreck, beatings, poverty, and now prison, with a possible death sentence looming.

But he had an unshakeable confidence that God would provide for his every need. Why? Because God had done just that.

Jesus teaches His disciples: "So I tell you, don't worry about the food or drink you need to live, or about the clothes you need for your body. Life is more than food, and the body is more than clothes" (Matthew 6:25). Everything they need—food, clothing, and shelter—will be provided by a generous Heavenly Father.

But that's not what I'm worried about. I have too many bills and not enough income. My kids need braces and the car is making funny noises.

The line between want and need is definitely blurred in our modern consumer culture. And all of us should probably step back and ask ourselves if we aren't making our lives a lot more complicated than they need to be.

But you are where you are. And God promises to meet you there and provide for you there. He doesn't want you consumed by worry. He does want you to honestly acknowledge your condition of need and then to open your heart to Him in trust.

He will take care of the rest and provide what you need.

Are you ready to receive God's provision of wisdom, resources, and blessings you need in your life?

> The Lord God is like a sun and shield; the Lord gives us kindness and honor. He does not hold back anything good from those whose lives are innocent.
>
> Psalm 84:11

REAL LIFE

The Least of These

NANETTE THORSEN-SNIPES

"But, Mom," said Jamie, my twelve-year-old, "you promised." Her usually expressive bright blue eyes dimmed.

I *had* promised that we'd visit the aquarium in Chattanooga, but unexpected household expenses drained every penny from our account. We couldn't even afford the gas to make the trip.

"I'm sorry, Jamie, the money just isn't there," I said.

And I didn't know when it would be. Jim and I had only been back in church a short while and we were learning how to live a godly life, which included tithing. But we needed to know how to handle what we made. We had even completed a workbook on finances, learning much about tithing, but hadn't put it into practice.

"I have an idea," said eleven-year-old Jonathan. "Why don't we have a garage sale?"

"You mean a junk sale? We don't have much to sell, you know." But the idea sprouted wings in my mind. If we could make enough for gas, our trip wouldn't have to be postponed.

Immediately, we put a garage sale into motion. We went through piles of clothes and other odd things. We found an old chest of drawers with a broken handle. Jim produced a rusted tiller that he no longer used, and the kids added stuffed toys they didn't play with. The kids gave up old bikes, and we found some webbed chairs that had seen better days. We added some old books and other odd items.

We filled up our carport, but it didn't look like much. I figured we'd be fortunate to make $100. Before Jim put up signs, we prayed. "Father, You know our need and our desire for short vacation. We ask for Your blessing on this sale. And Lord, we promise to tithe on anything we make."

That Saturday morning began with a bang—a bang on the door, that is. People started coming at 7:00 A.M. and came in droves until late that evening. What amazed us was the diversity of people who came. It was as though God handpicked people specifically for our garage sale.

We expected our neighbors, but we didn't expect the policeman who drove up in his squad car and bought a couple of our chairs. Or the handicapped woman who could barely walk, even with a cane, who wanted some books. We freely gave her what she wanted.

I was surprised to see a farmer drive up on his tractor. He bought the rusted tiller and came back later to pick it up. One woman who lived on the other side of town had gotten lost and ended up at our sale. She bought several things. Several people needed clothes and we lowered the price to a quarter apiece.

At the end of the day, we expected to make around $100, enough for gas. But when it was all said and done and we counted the money, we were shocked to learn we made almost $400, more than enough for our vacation.

And yes, we gave our tithe to the Lord before setting off on our adventure.

ACTION STEP

WRITE DOWN THE THREE OR FOUR THINGS YOU NEED MOST IN LIFE RIGHT NOW. THEY CAN BE FINANCIAL, EMOTIONAL, RELATIONAL, OR SPIRITUAL NEEDS.

PAUL SAYS, "DO NOT WORRY ABOUT ANYTHING, BUT PRAY AND ASK GOD FOR EVERYTHING YOU NEED, ALWAYS GIVING THANKS" (PHILIPPIANS 4:6). TAKE AN HOUR TO DO JUST THAT TODAY. SEE IF YOU DON'T FEEL BETTER!

PRAYER

Lord God, You have met my needs all my life. Thank You for Your faithfulness as my Father. God, please hear my heart today as I trust You with everything I'm facing.

THE POWER OF WORDS

WE ASSUME THAT WORDS DERIVE
FROM EXPERIENCE, BUT IT IS OFTEN
THE CASE THAT EXPERIENCING
IS A RESULT OF OUR WORDS.

Man's tongue is soft, and bone doth lack;
yet a stroke therewith may break a man's back.

BENJAMIN FRANKLIN

 TO THINK ABOUT

- Has there been someone in your life who has wounded you through their words?
- Likewise, has there been a person in your life who has enriched you through their words?
- Do your words heal and help—or hurt and hinder?

PROMISES

God will...

Bless you for resisting
the temptation to be
unkind
1 Peter 3:9

Use your words to give
others grace
Ephesians 4:29

Judge your words
Matthew 12:37

Bless you for your kind
words
Proverbs 22:11

Not Mere Words

BIBLE STUDY PASSAGE: JAMES 3

*What you say can mean life or death. Those who speak
with care will be rewarded.*

PROVERBS 18:21

John rightfully reminds us that we can't show love to
others by words alone, but that we must love with actions (1
John 3:18). James seconds that motion by telling us that "faith
that is alone—that does nothing—is dead" (2:17).

But these two biblical writers—as well as a host of
others—are also quick to tell us that words are a powerful
force, for both good and bad, in the world—

- *God created the world with words—"Then God said, 'Let there
  be light,' and there was light" (Genesis 1:3). The doctrine of ex
  nihilo declares that God created something from nothing.
  Matter sprang forth from words alone.*
- *Words reveal, reinforce, and can reform the condition of our
  hearts—"For as he thinks in his heart, so is he" (Proverbs 23:7
  NKJV). Which comes first—attitudes or actions? Usually*

60

actions! Don't like your thought life? Aren't satisfied with your heart? Change your words.

- *Words provide reconciliation and relationship—"Careless words stab like a sword, but wise words bring healing" (Proverbs 12:18). Don't settle for mediocre and broken relationships when your words can magically create new levels of understanding, trust, friendship, and intimacy. We get so caught up in what others should do, when we hold the key to life change at the tip of our tongues.*
- *Words unleash faith— "I can do all things through Christ, because he gives me strength" (Philippians 4:13). Based on verses like Matthew 17:20, some Bible teachers would go so far as to say that if you confess something with your lips, God is bound to make it come true. The point is that the nature of our words does have a highly predictive and efficacious quality. You can curse life with your words and bring it to pass, or choose to bless your life and the life of others.*

According to James, words are as powerful as a forest fire (3:5-6). Will you unleash a tidal wave of blessings in your life and the lives of those you love today?

As a tree gives fruit, healing words give life, but dishonest words crush the spirit.

Proverbs 15:4

REAL LIFE

Death and Life...

MAX DAVIS

Recently while watching a television talk show, I saw a young woman who had lost over 200 pounds. Sitting on the stage was this beautiful woman who looked like a model. When the before-and-after pictures of her were revealed, I was stunned. It was almost inconceivable that the woman onstage was the same woman in the pictures.

As the show progressed, she talked about how she accomplished her goal and what motivated her. It had been a long, arduous process, one that started in high school, and it would have been hard for any of us to stay the course.

Then the host introduced a young man, an acquaintance of hers, who had no idea why he was invited on the show. The woman wanted to thank him for what he had done for her. He, puzzled, was not aware of what he did to help.

She then began to disclose the story. She started by saying that losing the first 20 pounds was the most difficult. It had been so difficult that she felt losing 200 pounds would be impossible. After losing her first 20 pounds, she decided to go to her high school prom in the hope that someone would notice her. In her mind, however, she had already decided to quit dieting.

At the prom, no one danced with her or had anything to do with her. She was fighting back tears, thinking suicidal thoughts, when this young man spoke to her. All he did was tell her she looked nice and asked her if she had lost weight. According to her, he was a gentleman and treated her as a person with dignity. His few positive comments so touched her broken spirit that she decided in that moment to reach deep inside and continue pursuing her goal.

After the prom, they graduated and went separate ways until the show some three years later. It took her almost three years to lose 200 pounds. Now that she had accomplished her goal, she wanted him to see her and know how he had motivated her.

What am amazing story! Think about the power of those few encouraging words. Now think what might have occurred if this struggling young woman had received negative words that night. Instead of her broken spirit being mended, it would have been crushed. And the profound thing is the young man had not a clue of how transforming his words had been. Words are powerful! Benjamin Franklin wrote in 1740, "Man's tongue is soft, and bone doth lack; yet a stroke therewith may break a man's back."

The power of words can inspire. They can also crush. Solomon put it another way: "Death and life are in the power of the tongue" (Proverbs 18:21).

ACTION STEP

MAKE THIS AN ABSOLUTE POSITIVE AFFIRMATION WEEK. ON A SMALL SHEET OF PAPER, WRITE THE NAMES OF YOUR FAMILY MEMBERS AND OTHERS YOU SEE ROUTINELY IN THE LEFT COLUMN. NOW MAKE FIVE COLUMNS FOR THE NEXT FIVE DAYS OF THE WEEK. KEEP THIS WITH YOU AND MAKE A TICK MARK FOR EVERY POSITIVE AFFIRMATION YOU BESTOW UPON THAT PERSON. FOR FUN, ADD A BLANK TO ACCOUNT FOR STRANGERS. SHOCK SOMEONE AT THE GROCERY STORE WITH A CART OR LETTING THEM GO AHEAD OF YOU IN LINE.

PRAYER

Father God, I pray that only true, helpful things would ever come from my mouth. Give me a pure heart—and let it start with my words.

INTERCESSORY PRAYER

WE ARE CALLED TO EXTEND OUR FAITH AND OUR PRAYERS ON BEHALF OF OTHERS.

We must move from asking God to take care of the things that are breaking our hearts, to praying about the things that are breaking His heart.

MARGARET GIBB

 To Think About

- Have you ever sensed that someone is praying for you? Do you know someone who is praying for you?
- Who are you praying for right now?
- Do you believe that your faith and prayers can make a difference in someone else's life?

LESSON FOR LIFE

PROMISES

God will...

Hear your prayers
John 14:14
1 Peter 3:12

Reward persistence and
prayer
Matthew 7:7

Build up His people
Deuteronomy 28:9

Be among those gath-
ered in His name
Matthew 18:20

The Intercessor

BIBLE STUDY PASSAGE: ROMANS 8:26-34

By helping each other with your troubles, you truly obey the law of Christ.

GALATIANS 6:2

James, the head of the early church in Jerusalem, said that if anyone is sick, call for the elders of the church to lay hands on that person and anoint them with oil for their healing (5:14). Paul challenges the church in Galatians to "restore" to salvation the person who has fallen away from their Christian walk (6:15). Jesus sent all His disciples into the world to make new disciples in His name (Matthew 28:19-20). Throughout the Bible, we read that we really do need each other. Faith is not a solitary journey. The Church works like a body and each part is needed for it to work right (1 Corinthians 12:13-18).

One of the most dynamic expressions of this interrelatedness is intercessory prayer. This is when we add our faith on top of or in place of another person's faith. Maybe they have fallen into a pit of despair or a trap of sin and their faith is weak or non-existent. Maybe they are too young to be totally accountable or aware of an issue like illness or trauma in their life.   Whatever the case, one of the greatest ways we can express love and support to someone is when we ask God to act on their behalf—for healing, forgiveness, reconciliation, peace, and a myriad of other issues.   Amazingly, God will honor our faith through the Holy Spirit and impress our prayers on that person's heart.

Another incredible promise and source of comfort that we can cling to is that the Holy Spirit prays on our behalf, beyond our own understanding of our needs (Romans 8:26-27), and Jesus is our intercessor who constantly speaks to God the Father on our behalf (Romans 8:34).

Whatever your need—or the need of your loved one—be assured that your faith united with the faith of others creates miracles!

When a believing person prays, great things happen.
James 5:16

REAL LIFE

My Tiny Wooden Cup

GLENDA PALMER

A tiny wooden communion cup—a special gift—sits on my nightstand, and each night when I go to bed, it reminds me of God's presence. Our twenty-three-year-old son had just undergone surgery. The medical diagnosis: cancer—and the doctors didn't get it all.

Within a few days, his room was crowded with flowers and cards and caring, praying friends. My prayer partner sent a "heal"ium balloon to him.

What an encouragement my prayer partner was! She gave me some powerful scriptures which spoke to me of the all-sufficiency of Christ. She also gave me the little wooden communion cup with this note from another friend attached: "In Christ your child is my child and I shall shelter him in prayer as if he were my own. We are joining in communion for him each evening. The wee cup is your symbol of the covenant. You know of my love for you. Call anytime. I will not call you at present, but I will call to God who gives wisdom."

A few days later, several people gathered in our living room to anoint our son with oil and pray for his healing. My tiny wooden cup held the olive oil we used.

I wrote in my journal when I was in the middle of the fire:

We have joined the fellowship of Christ's suffering. With so many of His children crying out, "Abba, Father," on behalf of our son, I know He hears us and I know He is able. Our son is God's child and I am God's child, too. Our cups are empty but He is able to fill them. He alone is able. To Him be the glory.

Now, fifteen years later, as I look back on my son's illness, one of those "impossible situations" that come into our lives, I can still feel the pain I felt—but I also still feel the amazing grace and love that the family of God poured out on us during that time.

Each morning, I prayed and studied my Bible. Those words were my marching orders for the day. Hymns and praise songs were God speaking to me and me to Him. The Lord sent other people who were His angels to minister to me and pray without ceasing for Kent. God's grace! Yes! It was sufficient! It really was, whatever the outcome.

That was one of the hardest lessons that God wanted to teach me—"whatever the outcome." I needed to trust Jesus and love Him even if He chose to take our son to heaven. It took time to come to that place, but it was a place of peace. I wouldn't have come to that place without the diligent prayers of my brothers and sisters in Christ.

God answered our prayers with a yes. Our son is alive and well, married to a precious Christian wife, and father to our thirteen-year-old granddaughter. To Him is all the glory!

ACTION STEP

DO YOU HAVE A SPECIAL NEED IN YOUR LIFE RIGHT NOW? A HUGE DECISION?
A PHYSICAL AILMENT? A MONEY ISSUE? PROBLEMS WITH YOUR CHILD OR
SPOUSE OR A CLOSE FRIEND? GATHER A SMALL TRUSTED GROUP OF FRIENDS
TO UNITE WITH YOU IN PRAYER. PROVIDE THEM WITH SPECIFIC WAYS THAT
THEY CAN AGREE WITH YOU IN PRAYER.

PRAYER

*Thank You that even now the Holy Spirit is expressing to You the needs of my
heart and life. Thank You that Jesus Christ has interceded with You for the
forgiveness of my sins.*

RESTITUTION

EVEN THOUGH MAKING OUR SINS RIGHT TAKES GREAT EFFORT AND HUMILITY—IT SETS OUR SOUL AND SPIRIT FREE.

Prefer a loss to dishonest gain; the one brings pain
at the moment, the other for all time.

CHILTON

TO THINK ABOUT

- Have you ever stolen or lied about something that has weighed down on your heart?
- Did you attempt to right the wrong?   Was it even possible?
- What is the hardest thing about restitution—the "money" or the swallowing of pride?

PROMISES

God will...

Honor acts of restitution
Ezekiel 33:14-15

Bless those who are
honest
Psalm 37:37
Ezekiel 18:5-9

Develop your character
James 1:4

Forgive you
Matthew 26:28

A Bigger Heart

BIBLE STUDY PASSAGE: LUKE 19:1-10

When a man or woman does something wrong to another person, that is really sinning against the Lord. That person is guilty and must admit the wrong that has been done. The person must fully pay for the wrong that has been done, adding one fifth to it, and giving it to the person who was wronged.

NUMBERS 5:6-7

If you grew up attending church, maybe you remember singing a song about a small man named Zacchaeus: *Zacchaeus was a wee little man, a wee little man was he. So he climbed up in a sycamore tree for the Lord he wanted to see.*

We don't know a lot about Zacchaeus' background, but we do know he was a small man—but not just because of his height. Like the Grinch from Dr. Seuss, what was truly small was his heart. A corrupt tax collector, he stole from his own people on behalf of the Romans, and as a result, they despised him and he despised them.

But apparently, deep in his soul, Zacchaeus wanted some-

72

thing more—something bigger—in his life. He didn't want more money. He wanted to love and to be loved. That all became possible when Jesus entered his life.

He opened his home to Jesus—and those he once despised. Unlike the rich young ruler who loved money more than people, Zacchaeus also opened his pocketbook and paid back even more than he had stolen. This "wee" little man is still the model of restitution today.

One key symptom of an encounter with God is a desire to make things right with people you have hurt. It's not easy to pay back an old debt or give a long-overdue apology—but it's worth it to know that our lives reflect God's presence in our hearts.

Doing what is right and fair is more important to the Lord than sacrifices.
Proverbs 21:3

REAL LIFE

Just a Little Lie

JENNIFER JOHNSON

It was just a little lie.

A ridiculous, senseless fib.

I had just started teaching gymnastics. A local reporter interviewed me about my business. I was excited, thrilled, overjoyed. She took pictures and asked about my motivations and experiences. She asked if I'd received any special awards.

Suddenly, I panicked.

I lied.

It wasn't a *big* lie. I said I had won two spirit awards; in reality, it was one. I told her I'd been cheerleader of the year. Nope, not true. My lie wasn't that bad, so why did it bother me so much?

Because it hurt God. And I knew it.

I begged God's forgiveness, waiting with dread for the paper to be printed. I wrestled with Him about confessing, but I didn't make the call. I couldn't. I mean, it wasn't that big of a deal.

Right?

The following week, my friends ranted and raved over the article. My story took up half the page. A huge picture showed me assisting a girl with a tumble. The article was full of wonderful statements and comments. Then, I read the paragraph, the one paragraph that contained my lie. I wanted to vomit.

As I read my own words, I realized why the lie was so big. My purpose for starting the gymnastics business was not only to teach tumbling, but also to teach children about the Lord.

His words were all over my business walls. His music sounded from my stereo. I wanted them to know about Him, but I had begun my business with a lie.

I was miserable. Every time I opened my Bible, I felt prompted to make restitution. Every time I prayed, every time I went to church, every time I walked into my gymnastics shop, I knew I needed to make things right.

But, I didn't.

I went on with life. Eventually, my business closed. I went back to being a full-time mommy. I taught my children about the Lord. I taught Sunday school class. I participated in Bible studies. I wrote stories for the Lord. I continued to serve Him. But, in the recesses of my heart, when I was quiet and stood still and listened, I knew God still wanted me to make things right.

Nine years passed, and I came to the place in my relationship with God that I wanted freedom. I needed a clean slate so I could be a usable vessel in His hands. I had to obey. I called the editor of the newspaper and confessed. He not only thanked and forgave me, he shared a similar personal story of his own.

Maybe my confession wasn't as hard as repaying a million dollars, and it didn't make the front page of the paper. But I was freed, washed clean. I had trusted my Lord, and He restored my soul.

I can't think of a single thing worth feeling separation from my Lord, especially a little lie.

ACTION STEP

NOT ALL PAST WRONGS CAN BE MADE RIGHT. BUT IN MANY CASES, WE CAN RELEASE A HUGE BURDEN FROM OUR HEART BY PAYING BACK A DEBT WE HAVE INCURRED.

ASK GOD TO GRANT YOU CLARITY AND COURAGE TO BRING CLOSURE TO AN UNRESOLVED WRONG IN YOUR PAST.

PRAYER

God, thank You so much for Your patience with me. I ask You today for peace with my past—and the courage to do whatever it takes to make peace.

WORSHIP

WE WERE MADE FOR GOD—AND OUR SOULS NEED TO WORSHIP HIM IN ORDER TO THRIVE.

Worship is a thirsty land crying out for rain.

DWIGHT BRADLEY

 TO THINK ABOUT

- ☞ How long has it been since you worshiped God with your whole heart?
- ☞ How is your life different when you truly worship God—expressing love, honor, and gratitude to Him?
- ☞ Do you attend a church with a strong sense of worship?   Is Jesus lifted up?

LESSON FOR LIFE

PROMISES

God will...

Allow you to come into
His presence
Colossians 1:22

Be found by you as you
seek Him
Jeremiah 29:13
Psalm 34:4

Never leave you
Psalm 9:10

Bless those who seek
Him
Lamentations 3:25

The Way to Worship

BIBLE STUDY PASSAGE: PSALM 100

Psalm 100 is a short and beautiful poem that King David wrote for the people of Israel as part of their songbook. Not only are the words lovely to the ear, but they also teach us powerful truths about worship—

- *Worship should be enthusiastic. David says, "Shout to the Lord" (v. 1). That doesn't mean that every church and every believer must practice or appreciate the same worship style, but it does more than suggest that we need to engage our hearts in expressing our love to God.*
- *Worship is for everybody. David says that it is for "all the earth" (v. 1). Paul reminds us that on the Day of Judgment "every knee will bow" before the Lord (Philippians 2:10). Don't wait until then—worship God now.*
- *Worship should be joyful. David tells his people, "Serve the Lord with joy; come before him with singing" (v.2)—not because of duty and obligation.*
- *Worship recognizes that God is the Creator. David affirms that "He made us, and we belong to him; we are his people, the*

sheep he tends" (v. 3).   One of the biggest problems in modern society is a self-sufficient arrogance that thinks humankind is smart and good enough to take on the world without God. One look at the wars and other problems suggests otherwise.

- *Worship honors God's name.   David's call to "praise his name" (v. 4) is an important reminder in our profanity-laced culture that often uses God's name as an expletive.*
- *Worship is a group experience.   David says to "Come into his city with songs of thanksgiving" (v. 4).   In other words, even though we should worship God throughout the week, we should also gather with other believers to bring honor to His name.*
- *Worship expresses gratitude to God for His goodness.   David, a flawed man with a difficult life, can proclaim with all assurance: "For the Lord is good; His mercy is everlasting, And His truth endures to all generations" (v. 5 NKJV).*

That means His goodness endures to our generation and we, too, have much to praise God for!

But let all those who worship you rejoice and be glad.   Let those who love your salvation always say, "Praise the greatness of God."
Psalm 70:4

REAL LIFE

A Real Bear

KEVIN GALLAGHER

Can't remember what the argument was about.   But I do remember her saying that I was screaming at her.   Now that made me really mad.   I'm not a ranter and raver.   I never scream.

I guess the only thing that made me pause to consider what she said was that one of my colleagues at work had just told me the previous day that I was being a real bear to work with.   I didn't take it too seriously and just joked back that if you're going to be a bear, might as well be a grizzly.

Then I thought back a little further.   I had to agree that I really lost it the previous Monday night in a tennis league I play in.   It was a doubles match and one of our opponents really hooked us with a bad call on an important point.   I made a real scene—I felt justifiably.   But looking back seventy-two hours later, my posturing was not nearly as justified as it felt at the moment.

My wife finally agreed that I wasn't literally screaming.   But it didn't feel like much of a victory.   Add the other two events—and I'm suspecting quite a few others—of the past three days and I had to admit: For the past month or two, I was mad, short, irritable, cynical, sarcastic, prickly, mean.

No excuses, but I had been passed over for a promotion recently.   It wasn't a slam dunk situation where I absolutely should have gotten it.   I was younger than the other two final candidates, but I was disappointed.   Mad.   Not myself.

Yes, I was feeling very sorry for myself.

My five-year-old princess walked by with her blankie and asked if I was still mad at Mommy. I smiled outside—and felt terrible inside—and assured her, no, I wasn't mad at Mommy. She asked if I'd read a book to her. I said yes.

She pulled out her big blue Bible story book with lots of pictures that she likes so much. Of all things, our story that night was the story of the ten lepers. Jesus healed ten men. Only one went back and thanked Him and praised Him for all to hear.

I gulped for about the fifth time that night. I was in church every Sunday morning, of course, but I had to admit it, my heart wasn't in it. I wasn't thankful. I wasn't praising God. I understood my real problem behind a bearish attitude was not the job, but the lack of worship. I stopped right then and thanked God for getting my attention.

That next Sunday morning, no one sang louder, prayed harder, shook more hands and smiled more warmly, and listened more intently to the sermon than I did.

My wife still thinks I can be a grizzly bear, but this bear is happy, friendly, and praising his Creator.

ACTION STEP

ONE OF THE MOST BEAUTIFUL SCRIPTURE PASSAGES IS PSALM 100. AND ONE OF THE GREATEST SPIRITUAL DISCIPLINES IS MEMORIZATION. WHEN WAS THE LAST TIME YOU MEMORIZED GOD'S WORD? MEMORIZE ALL OR PART OF PSALM 100 TO TAKE WITH YOU THROUGHOUT THE DAY AS A SONG OF PRAISE TO GOD.

Shout to the Lord, all the earth. Serve the Lord with joy; come before him with singing. Know that the Lord is God. He made us, and we belong to him; we are his people, the sheep he tends. Come into his city with songs of thanksgiving and into his courtyards with songs of praise. Thank him and praise his name. The Lord is good. His love is forever, and his loyalty goes on and on. A psalm of David.

PRAYER

Dear God, You are my Creator. I shout for joy to You today.

A PARENT'S LEGACY

AS WE COMMIT OUR PARENTING
EFFORTS TO THE LORD, HE GIVES US
THE GRACE AND ABILITY TO BLESS OUR
CHILDREN IN SPECIAL, POWERFUL WAYS.

*The words that a father speaks to his children in the privacy
of home are not heard by the world, but, as in whispering-galleries,
they are clearly heard at the end and by posterity.*

JEAN PAUL RICHTER

TO THINK ABOUT

- ☛ What is the greatest challenge you face right now as a parent?
- ☛ What is the greatest joy in your life as a parent?
- ☛ How often do you go to your Heavenly Father in prayer for your children?

LESSON FOR LIFE

PROMISES

God will...

Crown your efforts with
success
Proverbs 16:3

Make you more like
Christ
Romans 8:29

Reveal himself to you as
you love your children
Matthew 25:21

Give you wisdom
James 1:5

Turn your kids' hearts
toward you
Malachi 4:6

Train Up a Child

BIBLE STUDY PASSAGE: DEUTERONOMY 6:19

*Train children how to live right, and when they are old,
they will not change.*

PROVERBS 22:6

After the children of Israel were delivered from slavery in
Egypt, had passed through the long, arduous journey of the wilderness, and were poised to move into the Promised Land, a great
challenge was given to the fathers that would bless not only their
own lives, but also the lives of their children and grandchildren.

- **Challenge #1: Be obedient**—*"Obey all his rules and commands I
  give you so that you will live a long time" (Deuteronomy 6:1-2). Do
  you want to raise obedient children? There's no better place to
  begin than your own obedience. There are no shortcuts on teaching
  the most important lessons in life. We have to model them.*
- **Challenge #2: Pursue God's truth**—*"Listen, Israel, and carefully
  obey these laws. Then all will go well for you" (6:3-4). In a society
  that celebrates moral relativism, we seem surprised when our children can't distinguish between right and wrong. Do you pursue*

truth by honoring God and His Word?

- **Challenge #3: Love God**—*"Love the Lord your God with all your heart, all your soul, and all your strength" (6:5-6)*. Raising great kids is really about being who God wants us to be. Do your kids know how much you love God?

- **Challenge #4: Teach God's Word**—*"Teach them to your children, and talk about them when you sit at home and walk along the road, when you lie down and when you get up" (6:7-9)*. In Old Testament times, parents would have a box on their doorpost that contained Bible verses to be read aloud whenever someone entered or left the house. Do you read Bible stories to your kids?

- **Challenge #5: Don't follow false gods**—*"Do not forget the Lord, who brought you out of the land of Egypt where you were slaves" (6:10-19)*. Even 5,000 years later, we are still faced with the temptation to follow false gods—gods of materialism and pleasure and success. Your children need to see a parent who is faithful to the one true God!

Raising children certainly isn't easy. You may be facing an uphill battle in your childrearing efforts. But with time, patience, consistency, humility, and a complete trust in God, you can bless your children beyond your imagination.

The father of a good child is very happy; parents who have wise children are glad because of them.
Proverbs 23:24

REAL LIFE

Just Like My Daddy

LINDA RONDEAU

Not able to have children of their own, my son and daughter-in-law adopted several children through the foster care system.   Each addition to the family has been considered a blessing—especially Joshua.   Nearly a year before, Joshua, who had been in foster care since early infancy, became free to be adopted.   When the agency called my son and daughter-in-law, who already had one adopted son and another whom they hoped to adopt, they opened their hearts to welcome Joshua into their burgeoning nest.   It was love at first sight when the affectionate youngster moved in.

When all the legal work was finally over, the family accompanied Joshua for his day in court.

The courtroom was silent, waiting for the judge to make a decision—a decision to determine not only where little Joshua would live, but also what his name would be.   The judge motioned Joshua to approach the bench.   From his austere heights, the magistrate pointed to someone in the room.   Each time, he asked Joshua, "Who is this?"

"Those are my brothers," Joshua said, referring to the other adopted children.   "That's Mommy," he explained as he pointed to my daughter-in-law.

Then the judge's attention focused on my son, who positioned Joshua in his arms, allowing the child to see the judge at eye level.   "And who is this man holding you?"

Joshua's eyes widened. He took his little hand and touched his father's face as he squealed in delight, "THAT'S MY DADDY!"

The judge, assured of Joshua's placement in a loving family, told John and Melissa that Joshua was now their legal son. Then the judge asked Joshua, "Do you know what your new name is?"

Joshua blurted out in excitement as he hugged his new father, "Joshua John Barringer, just like my daddy!"

Joshua takes great pleasure in imitating his father in just about everything. But his greatest thrill is to bear his father's name. For months after the adoption, Joshua said his name in a complete phrase: "I'm Joshua John Barringer, just like my daddy!"

Joshua's unabashed enthusiasm to become one with the family he loved made me think of my spiritual relationship to God. He holds me in His arms so that I can touch His face. He has given me the privilege to call him "Daddy, God." He asks me to be holy as He is holy. He wants me to emulate His example. Joshua's delight at his new name made my heart say to God, "I want to be just like You."

And maybe as I strive to be like my Heavenly Father, I'll leave a godly imprint on my children and grandchildren.

 ACTION STEP

YOU'VE SEEN PLENTY OF VERSE-A-DAY CALENDARS, E-MAIL NEWSLETTERS, AND BOOKS—WHY NOT MAKE YOUR OWN? CHOOSE A MONTH'S WORTH OF VERSES THAT HAVE SPECIAL MEANING TO YOU AND PLOT THEM ON A CALENDAR. READ A VERSE EVERY NIGHT AT DINNER OR BEDTIME. START OVER AT THE END OF THE MONTH!

 PRAYER

Heavenly Father, I know that You care about my kids more than I do. Help me today to point them toward You.

TURNING TO GOD FOR HELP

STRENGTH, DETERMINATION, AND SELF-RELIANCE AREN'T ENOUGH IN LIFE— WE MUST LEARN TO TRUST GOD.

When we call on God, he bends down His ear to listen, as a father bends down to listen to his little child.

ELIZABETH CHARLES

 TO THINK ABOUT

- Do you truly believe that God is still at work in the world today—in your life?
- Have you ever had to sit back and watch events unfold because there was nothing you could do to help? How did it make you feel?
- How would your responses in both good and difficult times be different if you had a deeper faith in God?

LESSON FOR LIFE

PROMISES

God will...

Help you
Hebrews 5:2

Send people to you
Psalm 20:2

Give you peace
Philippians 4:6-7

Be on your side
Psalm 118:7

Sometimes You Have to Pass the Ball

BIBLE STUDY PASSAGE: PHILIPPIANS 3:3-8

He chose what the world thinks is unimportant and what the world looks down on and thinks is nothing in order to destroy what the world thinks is important.

1 CORINTHIANS 1:28

Very few men have made a bigger splash in their chosen profession than Michael Jordan. He entered in the NBA in 1984 and averaged 28.4 points as a rookie. He led the league in scoring four of his first six seasons—but lacked what he wanted most, a championship. Interestingly, when he began scoring fewer points and depending more on others, he finally got what he coveted.

In life, we want to be masters of our destiny and our every situation. But too often we discover the reality that not all of life is under our control. A child's illness. Company problems. A downturn in the stock market. Conflict among neighbors.

The good news is that with trust in God we are never powerless or helpless. The Apostle Paul was a formidable character: He had his day's equivalent of two doctoral degrees (law and theology); he was a religious zealot who followed the letter of the law to a "t" (Philippians 3:6); he came from a wealthy and influential family (Philippians 3:5). But it was when he discovered that all his efforts and abilities weren't enough that he truly became a powerful force for God. He helped launch the Christian faith and turn the world upside down.

That's why he was quick to say, "The less I have, the more I depend on Him" (2 Corinthians 12:10). That's why this great orator would point out, "My teaching and preaching were not with words of human wisdom that persuade people but with proof of the power that the Spirit gives" (1 Corinthians 2:4).

God has blessed you with gifts and talents to make a difference in your world. But He's also created you with the need to depend on Him consistently.

Sometimes the greatest challenge in our lives is not to try harder but to trust more.

He will not forget the cries of those who suffer.
Psalm 9:12

REAL LIFE

No More Tears

JOAN CLAYTON

At first, we thought I had a rash.   Big, ugly red bumps appeared all over my face, but when they turned into ugly sores, I could hardly bear it.

I wanted to run away and hide from everybody.   To make matters worse, we lived on a poor farm and didn't have the money for doctors or medicine unless it was a matter of life or death.   We only had staples to eat.

It was bad enough to have a bumpy face, but all the girls in my class had the newest "in" clothes, their fashions out of the question for my poor family.   I tried to hide at school between classes so no one would see me.

I nearly broke down when I heard teenage girls in my Sunday School class whisper, "Why doesn't she ever have any new clothes?"

Kids made fun of me.   Some even called me "Scarface."

"What's the matter with her?" Dad asked Mom one day.

"She's crying over her face again.   Couldn't we use the cream money for a doctor?"

"Nope, just can't afford it.   She'll grow out of it."

But it seemed to get a lot worse and if I could grow out of it, I wished time would hurry up.   I felt embarrassed, miserable, and useless.

Every morning when I caught the bus even the little first graders started giggling.   I hated school.   Such pain I had never known in my sixteen years of life. Would it ever end?

One Sunday the preacher talked about prayer and how God always listens. I didn't think God would answer a teenage prayer about a bumpy face, but I needed a miracle, and in great desperation I prayed, "Lord, please do something about my face or send someone who can help me."

My Aunt Opal taught in the grade school adjacent to my high school. One day on bus duty, she saw me crying. Somehow she felt my pain. She arranged with my parents for me to stay in town with her for a while.

She took me to a dermatologist in a nearby city who specialized in acne. After several weeks, my skin began to clear up, and I started feeling like a person again. In fact, she turned "Cinderella" me into someone I liked. She restored my self-esteem. She bought me new clothes, and showed me how to use makeup. She even bought me perfume.

When I graduated from high school the next year, I held my head up high.

I shudder to think what might have happened to me had it not been for dear Aunt Opal. In my prayer I had asked for something or someone and God sent that "someone" just when I needed her.

I never had to cry over my face again, not ever.

ACTION STEP

WHAT ARE SOME SITUATIONS YOU ARE FACING THAT YOU SIMPLY DON'T HAVE THE RESOURCES TO SOLVE ON YOUR OWN? HAVE YOU SPENT TIME IN PRAYER PUTTING THESE SITUATIONS INTO GOD'S HANDS, ASKING HIM TO DO WHAT YOU ARE UNABLE TO?

WHY NOT TAKE A LONG WALK, GET AWAY FROM THE DISTRACTIONS, AND SPEND AN HOUR IN PRAYER?

PRAYER

Father, I try to do things on my own, but the truth is that I need You—all the time, in every situation. Please help me release all my burdens to You.

GOD'S PLAN FOR YOUR LIFE

ONE SIZE DOESN'T FIT ALL IN LIFE—DISCOVER WHAT GOD'S BEST IS FOR YOU.

God possesses infinite knowledge and an awareness which is uniquely His. At all times...I can realize that He knows, loves, watches, understands, and more than that, He has a purpose.

BILLY GRAHAM

TO THINK ABOUT

- What are different ways you have discovered who you are and who you are meant to be thus far in your life?
- Do you feel you are accomplishing specifically what God has set forth for you to do?
- How would you answer the question: "What do you want to be when you grow up?"

LESSON FOR LIFE

PROMISES

God will...

Enlighten you
2 Samuel 22:29

Show you the way you
should go
Isaiah 48:17

Speak your name
John 10:14-15

Show you new truths
John 16:13

Bless your perseverance
1 Peter 1:7

One Size Doesn't Fit All

BIBLE STUDY PASSAGE: 1 CORINTHIANS 1

From Paul, an apostle of Christ Jesus by the will of God. God sent me to tell about the promise of life that is in Christ Jesus.

2 TIMOTHY 1:1

One of the churches that St. Paul founded, the church at Corinth, proved to be a particularly troublesome burden on his heart. Yes, they were smart and sophisticated (1 Corinthians 4:10)—if you don't believe that, just ask them—but they had lots of problems, most notably a spirit of divisiveness—

- *They argued over who the best leader was (1 Corinthians 1:12).*
- *They argued over who was most spiritual (1 Corinthians 3:3).*
- *They argued over what the most important gifts were (1 Corinthians 12).*
- *They argued about the role of women in church services (1 Corinthians 14:33-34).*
- *They even argued over whether Paul was worthy of respect (2 Corinthians 10:10).*

Paul scolded them, shamed them, and even begged them to be united in love (1 Corinthians 1:10). And he used their spirit of contentiousness as opportunity to teach them about God's plans for us. He reminds the Corinthians that—

- *Each of us has unique gifts (1 Corinthians 12:28).*
- *Everyone's gifts are needed to complete the Body of Christ (1 Corinthians 12:12).*
- *We aren't to compare the value of our gifts (1 Corinthians 12:17).*
- *We aren't united because we are just like each other, but because we love each other (1 Corinthians 12:30-13:1).*

The good news for you is that God has made you one-of-a-kind unique—just like He has everyone else. Your job is not to be like others, but to discover and fulfill God's giftings for you—and to affirm and support others in that same quest.

Have you been missing out on God's best for you by trying to please everyone else?

Anyone who has the gift of serving should serve. Anyone who has the gift of teaching should teach. Whoever has the gift of encouraging others should encourage. Whoever has the gift of giving to others should give freely. Anyone who has the gift of being a leader should try hard when he leads. Whoever has the gift of showing mercy to others should do so with joy. Romans 12:7-8

 REAL LIFE

When God Says No

PAULA L. SILICI

My husband, Frank, and I suddenly faced a crisis: His company had transferred him out of state. Since he was nearing retirement age and we both didn't want to leave our beloved Colorado, we'd made the decision to temporarily live apart. Our awful separation was bad enough, but supporting two households soon presented a financial crisis as well.

Clearly, I needed to go back to work, but where would I find a job? Not having worked in over ten years, the thought of throwing myself into the job market again terrified me. At one time I'd been an efficient office manager for a prospering real estate company, but during the years of my absence, technology had advanced dramatically. Unfortunately, I hadn't kept up with the trends. I now felt terribly inept, and thoughts of facing job interviews gave me nightmares. So, after much prayer, I decided to apply at one of those safe, they'll-take-anybody temp agencies.

During my interview I was so nervous, I could barely type. At the end of the painfully dismal testing session, my embarrassed interviewer dismissed me with, "If something should come up, we'll call you."

I'd failed.

Back in the car, I sat for a long while, in tears, praying and asking the Lord why. Why had this happened to us, to me? Life had thrown us a huge curve, and it just wasn't fair. For days I'd asked Him for favor with the interviewer, that a good job would come from the interview. But that hadn't happened. Nothing was going right.

Then, in my watery misery I lifted my head. Beyond the parking lot lay a hilly field, and as I blinked away tears, I spotted a colony of prairie dogs, hundreds of them standing erect above their dens, surveying their domain. Suddenly, several raised their paws to heaven, as if offering hallelujahs in praise. Astounded, I heard the Lord whisper to my spirit, *They sow not, neither do they reap, nor gather into barns, yet your Heavenly Father feedeth them.*

In that moment, I knew things were going to work out. With the Lord's help, Frank and I were going to make it through this difficult time. God had said no to my prayers at that interview, but I could trust Him. He would open a door somewhere else.

As it turned out, I never did go on another job interview. Inspired by that heavenly "no," I began my own business instead, doing something I'd dreamed of doing for years. I am now a full-time writer and editor, doing work I adore and was truly born to do. Best of all, I am blessed to be my own boss, which means I can take my job with me whenever I want to visit Frank.

I may not have understood God's purpose during that horrid interview, but I do now. He knew exactly what He was doing. And like those prairie dogs, daily I praise and thank Him for His care. Hallelujah!

ACTION STEP

WE CAN'T LIVE IN A CONSTANT STATE OF INTROSPECTION, BUT SOMETIMES WE NEED TO STEP BACK FROM OUR OWN LIFE TO SEE HOW WE'RE DOING AND IF WE'RE ON COURSE.

Take a few minutes to do the following simple self-assessment:

NOT FULFILLED AT ALL---------------------------------- HIGHLY FULFILLED
AT WORK

NOT FULFILLED AT ALL---------------------------------- HIGHLY FULFILLED
IN FRIENDSHIPS

NOT FULFILLED AT ALL---------------------------------- HIGHLY FULFILLED
IN FAMILY LIFE

NOT FULFILLED AT ALL---------------------------------- HIGHLY FULFILLED
AT CHURCH

NOT FULFILLED AT ALL---------------------------------- HIGHLY FULFILLED
RELATIONSHIP WITH GOD

What are strength areas for you? What areas do you need to work on?

PRAYER

Dear Heavenly Father, I pray that today You would show me if I'm off track, and show me how to get where I need to be with You.   Lord, thank You for Your guidance and love.

FORGIVING OTHERS

ONE OF THE TRUE TESTS OF FAITH AND PERHAPS THE MOST POWERFUL EXPRESSION OF LOVE IS WHEN WE FORGIVE OTHERS.

To forgive is to set a prisoner free
and discover that the prisoner was you.

LEWIS B. SMEDES

 To Think About

- Have you ever forgiven someone but simply been unable to forget what they did to you?
- Why does God require that we forgive others?
- What gets in your way of forgiving others? Pride? Resentment?

LESSON FOR LIFE

PROMISES

God will...

Forgive you as you
forgive others
Matthew 6:14-15

Bless you as you forgive
1 Peter 3:9

Forgive kindly and
completely
Ephesians 1:7

See that love prevails
1 Peter 4:8

Forgive Us Our Debts

BIBLE STUDY PASSAGE: MATTHEW 18:21-35

*Let all bitterness, wrath, anger, clamor, and evil speaking
be put away from you, with all malice. And be kind to
one another, tenderhearted, forgiving one another, even
as God in Christ forgave you.*

EPHESIANS 4:31-32

Forgiveness is one of the most profound, pervasive, and
powerful teachings within the Bible—but also one of the most
difficult!

Are we required to forgive someone who abused us? An
unfaithful spouse? A person who hurts our child? One who
persistently takes advantage of us?

The clear and simple message of Jesus is that we are to
forgive—anyone and always. In the Lord's Prayer, our model
for prayer, Jesus teaches that it is only as we forgive others that
forgiveness takes hold in our own life (Luke 6:37). He knows it
will be difficult, but He reminds us that our love must extend
even to our enemies (Matthew 5:44).

But not everyone deserves to be forgiven! This is very

true. In fact, none of us deserve to be forgiven. This is what makes God's forgiveness of us so incredible and unexpected. As Paul said so eloquently: "Very few people will die to save the life of someone else. Although perhaps for a good person someone might possibly die. But God shows his great love for us in this way: Christ died for us while we were still sinners" (Romans 5:7-8).

Does this mean that the sin against me doesn't really matter? God never requires or asks us to minimize the pain and trauma of sin. God doesn't want us to be in denial as to what happened to us. And even after we forgive someone, it doesn't mean that all the earthly penalty is absolved. If someone has committed a crime, the legal system will still do its work.

Do I have to forget? Paul says that we aren't to remember and count someone's ways against them (1 Corinthians 13:5). That doesn't mean, however, we can just magically and instantly forget harsh and painful words or some other attack on us. But we do need to give even our memories to God and ask Him to bring healing over time.

What if I can't forgive? Again, present your situation and sorrow to God and trust that He is working in your life right now, even if the feelings aren't there.

Get along with each other, and forgive each other. If someone does wrong to you, forgive that person because the Lord forgave you.
Colossians 3:13

 REAL LIFE

The Question that Changed My Life

KITTY CHAPPELL

"I never lacked for anything as an only child, nor was I abused. But my parents never hugged me, never said they loved me, and never praised me. I am very successful—but still, no praise. They robbed me of something every child needs and it would have cost them nothing." Tears slipped beneath her lashes. "No, I *won't* forgive them!"

As a women's speaker who often talks about forgiveness, I was strangely touched by her tearful conclusion, recalling my own past resentments.

I was nineteen years old when I was asked to grant an unfathomable forgiveness.

Following church, an older woman stopped me to chat. Suddenly she asked, "Have you forgiven your father?"

My father was in jail, awaiting transport to the state prison for the premeditated attempted murder of my mother.

Mom's head wounds aren't even healed—how dare she even suggest forgiveness!

I mumbled something about how I didn't think I'd have to worry since my father would never ask my forgiveness for anything.

"You're probably right, but you still need to forgive him."

"Why should I do that? I've lived in fear all of my life for my mother and younger siblings. Dad bragged how he'd kill us, claim temporary insanity, and get away with it if we tried to leave. And he was sentenced to only three and a half years for premeditated attempted murder! Is that justice? No, I won't forgive him!"

"I understand, but you still need to forgive him."

"I'd like to know just who would expect me to do that!"

She replied softly, "God."

I glared at her, then ran down the steps.

Our house sold quickly and our hurting family moved from Texas to beautiful Southern California. *This is the new beginning I need—now I can be happy!* I thought.

But I wasn't. I felt moody, depressed, and angry. The woman's question popped into my mind, "Have you forgiven your father?" I tried to ignore it, but it seemed that every time I opened the Bible, it spoke of forgiveness. "Forgive, if you have anything against anyone." And again: "Father, forgive them," Jesus pled from the cross.

Even the books I read chided me. "Forgiveness is not an emotion," Corrie ten Boom wrote as a survivor of a World War II concentration camp, "it is an act of the will." She explained that she couldn't forgive through her own strength, but with God's help she did.

Finally I admitted one day, "Lord, I'd *like* to be able to forgive my father, but I have a problem—I don't want to. Can you change my wants—help me to *want* to forgive my father?" This became my daily prayer.

Some months later, I was overwhelmed with a sudden desire to forgive my father—I *really* wanted to. I whispered, "I forgive you, Dad, for everything!" My tears flowed freely, washing away all of my resentment.

I thank God for that woman's unwelcome question, for it led me to freedom.

ACTION STEP

IF YOU ARE STRUGGLING TO FORGIVE SOMEONE, THERE MAY NOT BE AN IMMEDIATE, SINGULAR MOMENT WHEN THE ISSUE IS RESOLVED FOR YOU. THERE CAN BE A SINGLE MOMENT, HOWEVER, WHEN WE COMMIT TO FORGIVING ANOTHER. ARE YOU READY? WITH GOD'S HELP, WILL YOU DO THAT TODAY?

PRAYER

Beyond my feelings, I extend to others the same forgiveness You lavished on me.

GIVING

GOD CALLS US TO SHARE FROM OUR ABUNDANCE WITH THOSE IN NEED—AND BLESSES US WHEN WE DO.

God has given us two hands—one to receive with and the other to give with. We are not cisterns made for hoarding; we are channels made for sharing.

BILLY GRAHAM

TO THINK ABOUT

- ⚿ When have you been blessed by someone's generosity?
- ⚿ When have you blessed someone else with your generosity?
- ⚿ Do you find it easier to give or to receive?

LESSON FOR LIFE

PROMISES

God will...

Be pleased with your
sacrifices
Hebrews 13:16

Love those who give
freely and joyfully
2 Corinthians 9:7

Be generous to you
Romans 10:12

Be pleased and glorified
by your work
Haggai 1:8

The Gift of Giving

BIBLE STUDY PASSAGE: ROMANS 12:1-10

*If there are poor among you, in one of the towns of the
land the Lord your God is giving you, do not be selfish or
greedy toward them. But give freely to them, and freely
lend them whatever they need.*

DEUTERONOMY 15:7-8

One of the true tests of our character is what we do with
our money.   Of course, God calls us to give a portion of our
income to Him through ministry (Numbers 18:28) and to also
give special sacrificial offerings to meet special needs as we
feel directed in our hearts (Numbers 15:3).   Paul does say that
some people have a special gift of giving (Romans 12:8), but he
also points out that God loves a cheerful giver (2 Corinthians
9:7), and Jesus himself drew attention to the meager—but
beautiful—gift of a poor widow as a true model of generosity
all of us should follow (Matthew 12:43-44).

When we are generous with our money above and beyond
expectations, a number of healthy emotional and spiritual
dynamics are fostered in our lives—

- We acknowledge that God owns everything and we have only been appointed as caretakers. The psalmist declares on behalf of God: "Every animal of the forest is already mine. The cattle on a thousand hills are mine" (Psalm 50:10).
- We clutch less tightly to what we can generate and become more aware that all good gifts come from God. James tells us: "Every good action and every perfect gift is from God" (James 1:17).
- We learn to trust and serve God with a pure heart. Jesus told His disciples: "You cannot serve both God and worldly riches" (Matthew 6:24).
- We receive the joy that comes from helping someone in need (Matthew 25:23).
- We become more confident and trusting, and begin to eliminate worry from our lives (Philippians 4:5-7, 17).
- We become better stewards in all areas of our finances; there is a strange paradox that the more we give the more we seem to have (Matthew 19:29).

And God can give you more blessings than you need. Then you will always have plenty of everything—enough to give to every good work.
2 Corinthians 9:8

The most important gift that God wants you to offer Him is your very life (Romans 12:1-2). Then He can teach you the wonderful truth that whatever we grasp and hoard, dries up and suffocates. Whatever we give freely and generously, takes off and soars.

REAL LIFE

Sweet Surrender

THERESE MARSZALEK

While scanning the church bulletin before Sunday morning service, a notice about a Russian refugee in need of furniture caught my eye. I sensed a strong impression: *Give them your dining set.*

You want me to give what? I thought. I had just placed a newspaper ad to sell our set so we could purchase one better suited to our needs. *God wouldn't tell me to give away our dining set, would He?* I thought. Surely He knew we needed the money and that we'd placed an ad in the newspaper, didn't He?

For the remainder of the day and into the night, I wrestled. The image of beautiful oak furniture stuck in my mind as a spiritual battle raged in my heart. *I'll donate it if it doesn't sell,* I considered. That compromise made me feel even worse.

The spiritual fog lifted as obedience to God became clear. When morning dawned, I surrendered to God's leading. Still in my bathrobe, I shuffled through cluttered papers for the church bulletin. I could hardly wait to make the call.

"Could your ministry use a dining room set?" I asked the person who answered.

Without hesitation, the woman told me about a Russian family of nine who fled to the United States with nothing. "They don't even have a table to eat on."

After making arrangements to pick up the furniture, she added, "Thank you for obeying what God asked you to do with your table."

How did she know? I had not shared my struggle of obedience. Overcome by

God's grace as I hung up the phone, tears of repentance fell to the floor.

The Russian man arrived with an interpreter the following afternoon. His eyes filled with tears when he saw their new furniture. Emotion-filled foreign words poured from his mouth while he wiped his wet cheeks.

"He says they've never owned anything so nice. He's thankful," the interpreter explained.

"Thank you, thank you," he said as they loaded the furniture into the back of his rusty truck. Watching them disappear around the corner, I pondered his tender display of gratitude.

The following Sunday, the Russian refugee leader approached me at church and asked, "Do you know anything about the family to whom you donated your furniture?"

"Not really," I said, interested in what she was leading to.

"That family is known for their generosity. When we visited Russia, we heard testimonies of their sacrificial giving. They had little, but willingly give of what they had." Then she beamed, "They prayed and asked God for the furniture they needed. They trusted God to provide."

I could only smile, knowing that words would open yet another floodgate of grateful tears.

As calls started coming in response to our newspaper ad, I contentedly chirped, "Sorry, the furniture is already gone."

God's furniture was exactly where He intended it to be. I was just a tool He used to get it there.

ACTION STEP

LOOK FOR A SPECIAL NEED IN YOUR COMMUNITY, NEIGHBORHOOD, OR CHURCH. ASK GOD TO IMPRESS ON YOUR HEART WHAT YOU CAN GIVE TO BLESS THAT PERSON OR FAMILY IN THEIR SITUATION. IF AT ALL POSSIBLE, MAKE YOUR GIFT IN SECRET AND KEEP IT BETWEEN YOU AND GOD.

PRAYER

I praise You, O God, who meets all my needs and lavishes me with all kinds of blessings. Thank You for enabling me to be generous with others.

TIME WITH GOD

IN THE HUSTLE AND BUSTLE OF LIFE, WE NEED STILL, QUIET MOMENTS TO BE ALONE WITH GOD.

*Every morning I spend fifteen minutes filling my
mind full of God; and so there's no room left for worry thoughts.*

HOWARD CHANDLER CHRISTY

TO THINK ABOUT

- 🔑 How often do you experience "quietness" in your life? How much is on purpose?
- 🔑 What are the biggest distractions in your life?
- 🔑 How would your life change if you spent even a little time each day in silent reflection?

LESSON FOR LIFE

Away from the Crowds

BIBLE STUDY PASSAGE: JOHN 4:1-11

Pray in the Spirit at all times with all kinds of prayers, asking for everything you need. To do this you must always be ready and never give up. Always pray for all God's people.

EPHESIANS 6:18

If you read through the four Gospels you can't help but notice how people—and crowds—were drawn to Jesus. If He went up a hill to pray alone, the crowds would be gathered below awaiting His return (Luke 4:42). If He jumped into a boat to slip off to the other side of a lake, word of His movements would race Him to the other side (Matthew 14:13). He interacted non-stop with military officers, widows, children, the seriously ill, the demon-possessed, religious leaders, close friends, prophets, and sinners.

At the beginning of His ministry at age thirty, despite having so much to do in such a short amount of time for His Father in heaven, Jesus pulled away from everyone to spend forty days in the wilderness to pray and fast. While alone,

Jesus was tested three times by Satan, but each time answered the challenge with scripture and a profound sense of His purpose in life (Matthew 4:1-11).

Again, at the end of his earthly life, Jesus pulled away from the crowds to pray alone in the Garden of Gethsemane (Mark 14:35-36).   It was there, with the agony of the cross just before Him, that He reaffirmed His most earnest desire: "Not My will, but Yours, be done" (Luke 22:42 NKJV).

If Jesus Christ sought solitude and quiet, how much more important is it for us?   We can come to the end of the day—or week or even month—and discover that we made no time at all to be alone with God.   Television, radio, meetings, chores, and a cacophony of other "noises" crowd out prayer and silent reflection.

You don't have to take a forty-day trip to the desert to create ways to spend quiet time alone with God.   In fact, once you recognize what distracts you from hearing God's voice, it's just a matter of giving yourself some quiet time.   Your soul will thrive as you pull away from the noise to hear the voice of your Father.

The Lord is close to everyone who prays to him, to all who truly pray to him.

Psalm 145:18

REAL LIFE

Sabbath Rest

JAN WILSON

"I can't do this anymore!"

The rosy sky reminded me that another beautiful weekend was nearly over. The sinking sun seemed to say: *You're not going to get everything done. Don't waste your time. Relax.*

I tried to refocus, but the words swirled on the page before me. *How many more times do I have to read this thing before it makes sense?* After reading it five or six more times, I threw the book across the room. My composure went with it.

What I wanted was a bachelor's degree in nursing, but I was falling apart at the seams trying to learn everything and do my best in school.

"Health professionals can have a deep impact on patient's lives," my physician friend had told me. "People are more receptive to spiritual matters during illness than at other times."

His words influenced my decision to attend nursing school, but I was more intrigued by his observance of the Sabbath. During medical school, he never worked, studied, or took examinations on Saturday. Even though our spiritual traditions differed, the concept of observing the Sabbath appealed to me now from a purely practical point of view. I was at the edge of sanity and looking over the cliff. Even prayer time had become something I had to cross off my daily "to do" list. I was fried, my brain was on overload, and I needed a solution.

I decided to set aside an entire day to rest, read scripture, and enjoy my family. No school work and no housework for twenty-four hours.

At first it was difficult to get off the treadmill. My mind rehearsed the list of things I should be doing as I attempted to relax. I worried that my grades would suffer from neglecting my studies on that day of rest.

Amazingly, to the contrary, rather than dropping, my grades improved—and so did my attitude! The evening following each Sabbath rest, my refreshed mind was eager to learn more. Study time was more efficient. There was room in my mind for new information. It took a near meltdown for me to realize I wouldn't die if I didn't pull a straight-A average. Now I was ready to admit that education was part of my life, but definitely not my whole life.

I experienced an even greater benefit. Though it took faith to put this Sabbath experiment into practice, after a while I saw my perspective change. Over time, I developed the deepening awareness that God deserves first place in my life. Observing the Sabbath helped me to refocus on God, the Source of my life.

When I prioritized my time according to God's plan, I experienced the inner peace and rest that I longed for. That peace carried over into my busiest days. What freedom it was to discover that God is the One who makes the dreams in my heart come true. I could work toward them, but their accomplishment was ultimately in His hands.

ACTION STEP

FASTING IS THE SPIRITUAL DISCIPLINE OF NOT PARTAKING OF FOOD FOR A SET PERIOD OF TIME IN ORDER TO DEVOTE OUR HEARTS AND MINDS TO SPIRITUAL MATTERS. BUT ABSTAINING FROM FOOD IS NOT THE ONLY PHYSICAL EXPRESSION OF FASTING. CONSIDER A ONE-, TWO-, OR THREE-DAY PERIOD OF NO RADIO, TV, OR OTHER "NOISE" IN YOUR HOME. (DISCUSS THIS WITH YOUR FAMILY FIRST!) REMEMBER, THE PURPOSE IS TO FOCUS OUR WHOLE HEART, SOUL, AND MIND ON GOD!

PRAYER

You speak to me through Your Word, and through pastors, and through books, but thank You, God, that You also speak to me in a quiet voice when I am silent before You.

GOD'S GRACE

GOD GIVES GOOD GIFTS
TO HIS CHILDREN.

*God loves and cares for us,
even to the least event
and smallest need of life.*

HENRY EDWARD MANNING

 To Think About

- Why is it so difficult to apprehend that God's forgiveness and blessings are free gifts?
- Do you ever slip into the subtle temptation of trying to earn and deserve God's favor?
- Do you ever struggle to accept God's grace into your own life?

LESSON FOR LIFE

PROMISES

God will...

Bless the merciful
Matthew 5:7

Be gracious to you
Luke 6:35

Care for the details of
your life
Psalm 139:3

Carry out His plan for
your life
Job 42:2

Riches of Grace

BIBLE STUDY PASSAGE: EPHESIANS 2:1-10

Let us, then, feel very sure that we can come before God's throne where there is grace. There we can receive mercy and grace to help us when we need it.

HEBREWS 4:16

Did you know God favors you? Not because are the smartest; not because you have lots of talents; not because you do many good deeds—though all of these characteristics may be abundant in your life!

No, God favors you out of His deep, abiding love for you, a love that is not contingent upon any effort you put forth. In fact, if you declared yourself to be God's enemy today, He would love you just as much.

God's grace is a wonderful reality that is available for you right now. Here's some aspects of grace that just might be what you need to hear today—

    • *Grace means God loved you and knew you before you were even born. The prophet Jeremiah says on behalf of God:*

"Before I made you in your mother's womb, I chose you. Before you were born, I set you apart for a special work. I appointed you as a prophet to the nations" (1:5).

- *Grace provides the gift of salvation, a gift that can't be earned. Paul says: "I mean that you have been saved by grace through believing. You did not save yourselves; it was a gift from God. It was not the result of your own efforts, so you cannot brag about it" (Ephesians 2:8-9).*
- *Grace is available to us when we are weak. Paul says: "So I am very happy to brag about my weaknesses. Then Christ's power can live in me" (2 Corinthians 12:9).*
- *Grace is sufficient for absolutely any need we have—whether health, finances, relationships, temptations, or any other need. Paul says: "My grace is enough for you" (2 Corinthians 12:9).*
- *Grace provides us with the strength we need to overcome temptation and live a victorious Christian life. Says Peter, "Jesus has the power of God, by which he has given us everything we need to live and to serve God" (2 Peter 1:3).*

Whatever need you have in your life today, be assured, God is on your side. He is ready and able to help you as you respond to Him with faith.

You were saved by faith in God, who treats us much better than we deserve.
Ephesians 2:8 CEV

A Special Christmas Story

JOANNE SCHULTE

We all have a collection of Christmas stories tucked into our memories, the greatest of which is the story of Mary and Joseph and the birth of Jesus, for it tells of God's great love in sending His Son to become our Savior. One of my favorite Christmas stories—a true story I've known for as long as I can remember—began in Pennsylvania in the early 1900s.

Viola was only five years old when she became a Christian, and in the years that followed, she felt God was calling her to be a missionary. At only fifteen years old, she decided to open a little mission church in an abandoned store in downtown Pittsburgh. Every Sunday morning, she rose early and hopped onto the streetcar that would take her to the little mission church where she shared God's Word with immigrant families.

During this time, Frank was a young seminary student, and along with a group of other seminarians, took his turn preaching at Viola's little mission church. He soon graduated, married, and started a family.

While working as a student nurse years later, Viola loved hearing the carolers sing in the halls of the hospital during the holiday season, and said to herself, *How wonderful it would be to give birth on Christ's birthday. If I ever have a child, I would like it to be born on Christmas.* She paused a moment to let that beautiful thought go deep into the recesses of her heart.

Her call to missions persisted, and after graduating from nurse's training, Viola went to Africa as a medical missionary. There she had amazing adventures and experiences, but never lived the love story she hoped for in the back of her mind.

Just how Frank and Viola became reacquainted remains a mystery, but it is known that their paths crossed again after Frank's wife passed away. There is even rumor of a marriage proposal that never arrived in the mail. What is known for certain is that on February 13, Viola's thirty-ninth birthday, they were united in marriage. Frank was forty-seven.

That same year, Frank and Viola rose early and opened their Christmas presents. And then at about noon that Christmas Day, a wonderful thing happened. God granted Viola her heart's desire. On that very day, the day we celebrate Christ's birth, Viola gave birth to a healthy baby girl.

Viola got her love story after all. It was a love story about Frank and Viola, but more importantly, it was about God's love in giving Viola the Christmas present she had wished for so many years before.

And it's a love story particularly close to my heart—Viola is my mother, and I am the baby girl who was born that Christmas Day.

ACTION STEP

IN THE OLD TESTAMENT, THE ISRAELITES WERE TO CELEBRATE GOD'S DELIVERANCE FROM EGYPT THROUGH A FEAST CALLED PASSOVER (NUMBERS 9:3). IN THE NEW TESTAMENT, THE CHURCH WAS TO CELEBRATE THEIR DELIVERANCE FROM SIN THROUGH PARTAKING OF THE LORD'S SUPPER (LUKE 22:19). WHAT ADDITIONAL REMINDER OF GRACE CAN YOU POST IN YOUR HOME TO KEEP YOU AWARE OF GOD'S FAVOR IN YOUR LIFE RIGHT NOW?

PRAYER

I can never thank You enough or ever hope to repay even a small portion of the ultimate gift You have given me through Jesus Christ's death and resurrection. I cling to Your grace today.

MONEY

WE NEED TO BE WISE WITH MONEY LEST IT DAMAGE OUR SOUL THROUGH THE TWIN EVILS OF GREED AND WORRY.

Do not value money for any more nor any less than its worth; it is a good servant but a bad master.

ALEXANDRE DUMAS

TO THINK ABOUT

- Is money an area of anxiety for you? One of contentment? One of overconfidence?
- Do you pay close attention to the way you spend your money?
- What significance do you think money has for your soul?

LESSON FOR LIFE

PROMISES

God will...

Take care of your needs
Philippians 4:19

Care for the poor
Psalm 72:12

Help you obey Him
Philippians 2:13

Bless those who are
generous
Proverbs 22:9

Our Daily Bread

BIBLE STUDY PASSAGE: MATTHEW 6

And don't make me either rich or poor; just give me enough food for each day. If I have too much, I might reject you and say, "I don't know the Lord." If I am poor, I might steal and disgrace the name of my God.

PROVERBS 30:8-9

In the Sermon on the Mount, Jesus calls us to steer clear of making money and things the highest priority in our lives (Matthew 6:24 and 32-33). When we obsess over money, we encounter several problems: We become distracted from God; we don't love others as we should because of greed and envy; and we become unhappy and ungrateful because we focus on what we don't have instead of what we do have.

Obviously, God cares a lot about what we do with our money. He calls us to give a portion of our income off the top to Him (Malachi 3:10). Paul strongly urged the Corinthian congregation to meet the needs of other churches: "Each one should give as you have decided in your heart to give. You should not be sad when you give, and you should not give

126

because you feel forced to give. God loves the person who gives happily."

Outside of the Bible, perhaps the wisest words ever uttered about money come from the great eighteenth-century British evangelist and social reformer, John Wesley—

Make all you can;
Save all you can;
Give all you can.

To do those three things requires hard work, self-control, and generosity, three virtues that God rewards—and three virtues that will solve almost all money management problems.

As in all areas of life, what matters most is our level of trust in and honor for God: "Trust the Lord with all your heart, and don't depend on your own understanding. Remember the Lord in all you do, and he will give you success" (Proverbs 3:5-6). As we seek to honor the Lord by asking for His counsel and following His guidelines for money and work, He will meet our needs.

The thing you should want most is God's kingdom and doing what God wants. Then all these other things you need will be given to you.
Matthew 6:33

REAL LIFE

Drained by Debt

EILEEN KEY

I forced a smile as the checker greeted me and started scanning my groceries. "Did you find everything you needed?"

I nodded, my eyes on the register.

An ache shot through my chest as the total rose—and rose. Finally, the last item slid across the counter, and I sighed. One more time, we'd squeaked by. I wheeled the groceries to my car.

Before I entered the house, I checked my mailbox. A cold fear grabbed me when I saw an envelope from my bank. An overdraft notice. Again.

I started dinner for my three children. The spaghetti sauce bubbled and splattered on the stove. My kids chatted about their day. I looked at the meal. No steak and lobster. We lived a middle-class lifestyle: clothes for three children, pizza, movies on Fridays. Why couldn't I make ends meet?

After my divorce, our suburban lifestyle seemed impossible to live on a teacher's salary and child support. A part-time job was out of the question. There was no "part-time."

After dinner, everyone dispersed. In my bedroom, I slumped to the floor and pulled my Bible out to read a Psalm. I poured out my heart to God.

Father, I can't keep up. I'm drowning and need direction. Sobs left me emotionally exhausted. Worry crept in and cloaked me.

"Mommy?" My eleven-year-old, Rachel, surveyed the pile of mail, looked at my red-rimmed eyes, and hugged me. "It's okay. Remember the Bible says God is our provider."

The following morning, I flipped open my Bible and landed on Matthew 6:24: "No man can serve two masters. You cannot serve both God and money."

Was I serving money? Financial worries consumed my thoughts and took my eyes from the Lord. Evidently I was.

The afternoon mail brought a bright yellow circular from a Christian credit counseling group. I read it, and my heart soared. God had given me direction. I called the number and set up a time to meet with a counselor. They had a solution. With their help, I set up a budget and a debt repayment plan with realistic goals. I also reassessed my priorities.

I didn't like having to forego the newest and best for my kids, but I soon realized my children didn't care. It was easier to live with the less-stressed Mom. We discussed our budget and made changes, and they happily complied.

Soon I noticed I didn't cringe at the arrival of the mail. The counseling group had direct-drafted my bank account and made my payments smaller collectively than they had been before. Relief flooded me each month as I watched the balances recede.

Four years later, I climbed out of the money pit with God's help and the encouragement of a non-profit organization. I became debt free. Today I don't work to pay MasterCard. Instead, I work to serve the greatest Master of all.

ACTION STEP

GRAB YOUR CHECKBOOK AND TAKE A LOOK AT HOW YOU'RE SPENDING YOUR MONEY. ARE YOU SPENDING IT TOO FAST? ARE YOU SPENDING IT UNWISELY? OR DO YOU NEED TO LEARN TO BE MORE GENEROUS AND GIVE SPONTANEOUSLY TO YOUR LOVED ONES?

ON A SMALL CARD, WRITE OUT: "MY GOD WILL USE HIS WONDERFUL RICHES IN CHRIST JESUS TO GIVE YOU EVERYTHING YOU NEED" (PHILIPPIANS 4:19) AND PLACE IT IN YOUR CHECKBOOK WHERE YOU'LL SEE IT EVERY TIME YOU WRITE A CHECK. OVER THE NEXT MONTH, EVERY TIME YOU MAKE A PURCHASE, ASK GOD TO HELP YOU TRUST AND OBEY HIM WHEN IT COMES TO MONEY.

PRAYER

Father God, You have been so generous with me, and I'm grateful. Help me honor You with the way I spend my money.

SERVING GOD

ONE OF THE GREATEST SOURCES OF PERSONAL JOY IS WHEN WE REACH OUT TO OTHERS IN LOVE AND SERVICE

You who have received so much love share it with others. Love others the way God has loved you, with tenderness.

MOTHER TERESA

TO THINK ABOUT

- Who are people who have modeled a lifestyle of service for you?
- In what ways are you serving others and your church today?
- What gets in the way of servanthood for you?

LESSON FOR LIFE

PROMISES

God will...

Produce fruit in your life
John 15:1-5

Exalt those who humble
themselves
1 Peter 5:6

Reward your persistence
Galatians 6:9

The Towel and Basin Society

BIBLE STUDY PASSAGE: JOHN 13:1-20

If I then, your Lord and Teacher, have washed your feet, you also ought to wash one another's feet. For I have given you an example, that you should do as I have done to you.

JOHN 13:14-15

One of the issues that most mattered to Jesus' disciples was who of them was the most favored and important to Jesus. In fact, two of the disciples, James and John, asked their mother to help them assume the seats of honor in Jesus' kingdom. Her request to Jesus was: "Grant that these two sons of mine may sit, one on Your right hand and the other on the left, in Your kingdom" (Matthew 20:21).

Jesus' response was that she didn't know what she was asking. She and her sons were interested in the trappings and benefits of power, but not the sacrifice. Otherwise, these sons of Zebedee could have been on Jesus' left and right when He prayed in the Garden (Matthew 26:40-46). Instead, they slept. They could have been on His left and right when He was

132

arrested (Mark 14:50). Instead they fled. They could have
been on His left and right when He hung on a cross (Matthew
15:27, Luke 23:49, John 19:16-19, 26). Instead, they stayed in
the crowd.

When Jesus taught His disciples the true meaning of
greatness, he taught with a towel and basin. He washed their
feet—the duty of a house servant. Peter, still unable to
comprehend the object lesson, initially refused to let Jesus
lower Himself in such a way.

We live in a competitive and self-aggrandizing world.
Examples of humility, kindness, helpfulness, and caring for
others first—servanthood—are hard to find.

Great is the reward, the sense of purpose, the self satisfac-
tion of one who follows the Master's example as a member of
the "Towel and Basin Society."

I mean that I want us to help each other with the faith we have. Your faith will help me, and my faith will help you.
Romans 1:12

Ministry is More than Clowning Around

THERESE MARSZALEK

Keep me humble, Lord, my husband, Tom, prayed regularly. I knew God had a sense of humor when I saw Tom's name on the signup sheet for clown ministry training.

"I asked God to keep me humble, so He makes me a clown? That's not exactly what I had in mind," Tom laughed.

After learning about clowning, costumes, face painting, and balloon animals, Tom used his ministry training at birthday parties and church functions.

When we moved from Seattle to Spokane, Tom hung up his clown costume and packed the makeup and balloons away. Although the endless hours Tom had given to brightening people's lives blessed many, he gratefully assumed the season of humility in serving the Lord through clowning was over.

Tom realized his clown days were not over when the pastor's wife called. "I hear you've been a clown in the past," she said. "Would you be willing to dress up as a clown and entertain the kids that come to the church picnic next week?" Tom agreed to her request, although I knew he wasn't excited about the idea.

On the day of the church picnic, Tom woke with a headache brewing. By afternoon, he was suffering from a full-blown migraine. Although I suggested he cancel his clowning obligation, he insisted on fulfilling his commitment.

I watched Tom cringe as he painted his face and pulled on his size-seventeen yellow shoes. Feeling less than able to perform, he headed to the picnic with pockets full of balloons and candy. I knew he wasn't looking forward to entertaining anyone, especially loud children.

All afternoon children crowded around Tom, pulling his red nose, squeaking his horn, and grabbing balloons out of his pockets. Kids waited in long lines for Tom's carefully formed sword or animal shaped balloons.

Tom's pain showed in his strained eyes, although a faith-filled smile remained on his face. He didn't mention his suffering to anyone, but continued to bless the children.

As the church picnic wound down, a mother from our church family told Tom that her son had been hospitalized with a heart condition. "Would you be willing to visit Andrew at the children's hospital today?" she asked.

"Sure," Tom said. Tom had been looking forward to going home so he could collapse into bed, but was touched by this mother's request.

Tom drove to the hospital, knowing Andrew needed a touch of God's joy. Pressing through his pain, Tom sowed into this young life, strengthened and equipped by God's grace and power.

When I visited Andrew several days later, he jabbered endlessly about the funny clown that had visited him in the hospital. God's love, poured out through a weakened vessel like Tom, made a difference in little Andrew's life.

Seeing how God fueled Tom with His love to serve others reminded me of the song I learned as a child: "They will know we are Christians by our love!"

ACTION STEP

IS THERE AN AREA OF YOUR CHURCH YOU'D LIKE TO GET INVOLVED IN, BUT HAVEN'T GOTTEN AROUND TO IT? FIND LAST SUNDAY'S BULLETIN AND LOOK FOR A MINISTRY THAT NEEDS YOUR HELP, THEN MAKE THE CALL THAT WILL START YOU ON THE PATH TOWARD SERVING.

IF YOU'RE ALREADY INVOLVED IN A MINISTRY, SPEND THIS SUNDAY REFLECTING ON THAT AREA OF YOUR LIFE—ARE YOU EXHAUSTED? DO YOU NEED TO SCALE BACK? ARE YOU HOLDING BACK—DO YOU FEEL GOD PROMPTING YOU TO UP YOUR COMMITMENT? SET GOALS FOR YOURSELF FOR THE NEXT WEEK, MONTH, AND YEAR.

PRAYER

Thank You, God, for sending Jesus into my life and heart with the gift of salvation. Help me to honor that gift through service to others.

USED BY GOD

EVEN WHEN WE ARE UNCERTAIN ABOUT OUR ABILITIES, GOD HAS CONFIDENCE IN US AND CAN DO GREAT THINGS THROUGH US.

It is not the possession of extraordinary gifts that makes extraordinary usefulness, but the dedication of what we have to the service of God.

FREDERICK WILLIAM ROBERTSON

 TO THINK ABOUT

- ⚷ Have you ever felt called by God to help someone or do something good, but were too afraid to try?
- ⚷ Do most of your friends have a healthy self-esteem, or are they good at faking it?
- ⚷ What is something great you would like to accomplish in life? Have you talked to God about this?

LESSON FOR LIFE

PROMISES

God will...

Reward your efforts
1 Corinthians 3:8

Prepare you for good
works
Ephesians 2:10

Delight in you
Psalm 147:11

Deal with you according
to your heart
1 Samuel 16:7

Just As You Are

BIBLE STUDY PASSAGE: EXODUS 4:1-17

But Moses said to the Lord, "Please, Lord, I have never been a skilled speaker.   Even now, after talking to you, I cannot speak well.   I speak slowly and can't find the best words."

EXODUS 4:10

We live in a dog-eat-dog world.   It sometimes *seems* like only the most athletic, best looking, and most near perfect get noticed.   Many of us question our abilities and are fearful about testing our wings and attempting all that God has called us to do.

If you ever struggle with healthy self-confidence, note that one of the greatest leaders in all of history, Moses, had the same hang-up.   When God called him to lead the children of Israel out of Egyptian bondage, Moses was full of excuses. *They won't listen to me.   I stutter.   Send my brother.*   Maybe it was the trauma of separation from his parents as a baby and being adapted into a "foreign" culture.   Maybe it was the guilt of things he'd done in his youth or being raised as a prince while his own family served as slaves. Whatever the reasons, Moses had deep fears about whether he was good enough.

But God was patient with him and didn't demand that Moses work on his speech or schmooze with the right people to make him a more effective leader. When Moses trusted God and stepped out on faith to confront the Pharaoh and help forge a free nation, he took to heart God's promise to him: "I will help you speak, and I will teach you what to say" (Exodus 4:12).

Yes, we should continually improve ourselves. It's good to strive for excellence in our lives. But we shouldn't forget that God often gives us things to accomplish that are beyond our abilities and can use us no matter what seems to stand in the way. No matter how much "work" you think you need right now, be assured that God can use you just as you are.

God has made us what we are. In Christ Jesus, God made us to do good works, which God planned in advance for us to live our lives doing.
Ephesians 2:10

REAL LIFE

You're So Pretty

TSGOYNA TANZMAN

At twenty-two, I graduated with a Master's degree in speech pathology and started working with elderly stroke patients. Being petite and "young," I frequently heard comments like, "You're so pretty. Isn't she cute?" *Won't anyone take me seriously? Don't they know I'd graduated with honors and published a scientific paper in a journal of my peers?*

My job as a therapist was to help a patient recover his communication skills—to teach him or her to speak again. I'd arrive dressed for success with my protocols and treatment plans. I'd review previous assignments and leave homework for our next meeting. At the session's end I'd record detailed notes sprinkling liberal amounts of jargon and impressive statistics, making sure that Medicare knew I was competent and deserving of my fee.

But beneath this veneer of professionalism bubbled a nagging feeling of fraudulence. Was I just a cute little visitor, not a real therapist? I cared about my patients, but was that enough? My supervisor's evaluation confirmed my worst fears.

"Ms. Unger demonstrates adequate skill as a speech pathologist. Although her special strengths include record-keeping and her warmly supportive relationship with patients, she needs to make therapy tasks more functionally relevant."

"Adequate." Adequate to me is nothing. Non-descript, barely passable. *Maybe I'm not cut out for this type of work. I obviously stink at it. Maybe I should teach aerobics—be with young, healthy people. Do something where I can see results quickly.*

So after five years of practicing as a speech pathologist, I gave it all up for a leotard. During my phase of perfecting myself physically, I developed a colon problem and found myself in the hospital.

I was post surgery, groggy from a morphine drip and tethered to various IV tubes, when a nurse came to check on me. The curtain around my bed swished. And then I heard it, clear as a blue sky the day after a rainfall, God's voice dripping in southern sweetness: "Good morning, sugar. How ya' feelin'?"

I strained to open my eyes. Without thought, the words slipped from my parched lips: "You're so pretty."

In the presence of this angel, my vulnerability lifted. I felt safe. I felt hope.

Finally I understood what my patients had meant as they struggled to speak the words, "You're so pretty." It wasn't what they saw, but what they felt: hope.

Not long after I left the hospital, I returned there, staying another fourteen years—not as a patient, but as a speech pathologist. "Adequate" skills improved to "superior," and then I heard God's voice again. Only this time it gurgled. I'd become a mother and decided mothering was my new career. As I cradled my newborn daughter, she snorfled and snuffled, but I'm pretty certain she meant, "Mama, you're so pretty."

ACTION STEP

WHAT IS ONE THING YOU WANT TO DO, BUT AREN'T QUITE SURE YOU CAN? SING OR PLAY AN INSTRUMENT WITH YOUR CHURCH WORSHIP TEAM? LEAD A SMALL GROUP? TAKE ON A NEW ROLE AT WORK? DETERMINE ONE STEP YOU CAN TAKE FORWARD, AND PRAYERFULLY GO FOR IT THIS WEEK!

PRAYER

Lord, thank You that You use us to do big things in the world. Help me hear Your voice and do all that You've called me to do.

SHARING GOD'S LOVE

THE BEST WAY TO SHARE YOUR FAITH WITH OTHERS IS BY LIVING A LIFE OF OBEDIENCE AND LOVE.

*Nobody will know what you mean
by saying that "God is love"
unless you act it as well.*

LAWRENCE PEARSALL JACKS

TO THINK ABOUT

- ⚷ Has there been someone in your life who helped you have more faith in God because of the way they conducted their life?
- ⚷ Do your attitudes and actions draw people closer to God or push them away?
- ⚷ How can you show more love to someone who needs to know God?

LESSON FOR LIFE

PROMISES

God will...

Lead people to himself
1 Timothy 2:4

Give you love for others
1 Thessalonians 3:12

Bring people close to
Him
Psalm 5:7

Use your example
Daniel 12:3

Love Each Other

BIBLE STUDY PASSAGE: 1 JOHN 2:7-10

All people will know that you are my followers if you love each other.

JOHN 13:35

When Peter wrote to a small group of Christians who were persecuted and made fun of for their faith, he said: "Always be ready to answer everyone who asks you to explain about the hope you have" (1 Peter 3:15).

That means that all of us should be prepared to tell others how we know God is real and has made us into a new person through Jesus Christ. Have you ever thought through what you would say to someone who wants to have a personal relationship with God? Do you have a couple of Bible verses memorized that you could share with them? Would you be ready to pray with them?

But just as important as having words to say is the way we live our lives. Many people have quit going to church or attending a Christian youth group because of the bad attitudes and activities of those who call themselves Christians. Jesus tells His disciples that the easiest way people will know that they have a real and powerful relationship with God is by how they love one another.

One of the greatest and most powerful expressions of love is found in 1 Corinthians 13, where Paul says: "Love is patient and kind.   Love is not jealous, it does not brag, and it is not proud.   Love is not rude, is not selfish, and does not get upset with others.   Love does not count up wrongs that have been done" (vv. 4-5).

How about you?   Do you show love to your family through your words and your actions?   To your friends?   Are you helping the people around you draw closer to God?

But when the Holy Spirit comes to you, you will receive power.   You will be my witnesses—in Jerusalem, in all of Judea, in Samaria, and in every part of the world.
Acts 1:8

The Rocking Chair Girl

EILEEN ZYGARLICKE

She sat in the chair and rocked in silence for five days. No words. No acknowledgement that we existed. Nothing. For eight hours a day, she sat in the chair, sullen, morose, and mad, rising only to eat meals. Her name was Jamie and she was our newest foster teen.

Separated from her family for two years, she came to us from a group home at the age of fifteen. Change is always difficult for foster teens, and Jamie was no exception.

My husband and I prayed about how to react to this silence and received wise words from Him in reply. We loved her and talked to her, despite her lack of response. After five days, we finally broke through—Jamie began to respond. A few words here and there turned into sentences, which morphed into conversations. After a few weeks, Jamie was laughing and joking with us as though she'd lived with us her whole life.

During her stay, the rocking chair became her refuge. Known to all as "Jamie's Chair," it was a place of comfort for her. While sitting in the chair late at night, Jamie would begin to open up and ask probing questions. Why had we talked to her when she first came to us, despite her icy silence? Why did we eat together as a family? Why did we tell her we'd pray for her for tests at school? Why did we care?

One night, my husband made a passing comment about something God had shown him about Jamie. Jamie clamored to know what God had said, who He was, and why He cared. We were able to share our faith with her, telling her of the One who loved her more than she could know.

Periodically, Jamie would ask more questions about God. We never pushed our faith on her, but loved her and reminded her often of God's love for her.

Months passed, and it was time for Jamie to move with her family to another state. Filled with apprehension, she made us promise to keep in touch. She called periodically, filling us in on her newest boyfriend, wanting my husband and me to approve. We teased and laughed and always told her how much we and God loved her.

One day Jamie called, filled with excitement. "I've got a new boyfriend," she happily divulged. "You'd like him. He goes to church and takes me with him. He doesn't drink, smoke, or swear. And he's really nice to me." All of these were firsts for Jamie.

She called again a few weeks later. "I finally get it," she said through tears. "I finally understand that stuff you told me about God's love. You may have thought I was hopeless, but I finally get it."

We talked and cried, then said our good-byes. As I hung up the phone, I looked at the empty rocking chair and thought of the miracle God had done in her life. The journey had taken years, but our rocking chair girl was finally truly in the family.

ACTION STEP

ONE OF THE SIMPLEST WAYS TO SHARE WITH SOMEONE HOW THEY CAN KNOW GOD IS CALLED THE ROMAN ROAD—

- ROMANS 1:20-21
- ROMANS 3:23
- ROMANS 5:8
- ROMANS 6:23
- ROMANS 10:9-10
- ROMANS 10:13
- ROMANS 11:36

TAKE A MINUTE TO WRITE OUT THE ROMAN ROAD AND TUCK IT SOMEWHERE WHERE YOU'LL HAVE IT ON A MOMENT'S NOTICE. PRAYERFULLY LOOK FOR OPPORTUNITIES TO SHARE THIS MESSAGE OF SALVATION!

PRAYER

Father, thank You for saving me. I ask You today for the courage to tell others how good You are and the strength to share Your love.

YOUR FUTURE

WHEN WE ARE GOING THROUGH TOUGH TIMES WE MUST REMEMBER THAT OUR FUTURE IS IN GOD'S HANDS.

Life is God's novel. Let Him write it.

ISAAC BASHEVIS SINGER

TO THINK ABOUT

- Have you ever been so discouraged that you didn't believe even God Almighty could help you?
- Have you ever sensed God leading you to take a new path that will change your future?
- Are you trusting your future to God right now?

PROMISES

God Will:

Reveal himself
Proverbs 2:3-5

Bring success
Proverbs 16:3

Hear your prayers
1 John 5:14

Carry out His plan for
your life
Jeremiah 29:11

A Future and a Hope

BIBLE STUDY PASSAGE: JOHN 10:10-16

"I know what I am planning for you," says the Lord. "I have good plans for you, not plans to hurt you. I will give you hope and a good future."

JEREMIAH 29:11

Jeremiah is known as the "weeping prophet." Imagine losing absolutely everything you hold dear—your family, home, country, church, and maybe even your faith. Jeremiah anguished over what had happened to his people. King Nebuchadnezzar had conquered the Kingdom of Judah, destroying the walls of Jerusalem and the temple built by Solomon. The strongest and most educated were led as captives to serve the conquering king. They left behind all they loved, smoldering in ruins.

This young man of God preached to the Hebrew exiles, who now lived in the foreign country of Babylon, along the banks of the Tigris River.

Like Job who had lost future and family; like Joseph and their Hebrew ancestors who were captives in Egypt, despair reigned in the lives of the Israelites—their hope was lost. How could they think of themselves as God's chosen people under such circumstances?

In the midst of this hopelessness, this young prophet, Jeremiah, called to speak for God at an early age, dried his eyes and boldly proclaimed a new promise—that God had a future filled with hope for these people. That promise did come true for the Hebrew children, and the promise still echoes and holds true today, no matter what the situation in which you find yourself.

Do things look bleak in your life right now? Are you flooded with insecurity about the future? Just as God had a plan for His people thousands of years ago, He has a plan for you—a good, pleasing, and perfect plan. And He is trustworthy to make that plan happen.

Lord, I know that a person's life doesn't really belong to him. No one can control his own life.

Jeremiah 10:23

151

REAL LIFE

Greener Pastures

GARRETT FRYE AS TOLD TO RONDI FEYEREISEN

The pastures of my life were not green anymore. Despite the loving wife, healthy children, beautiful new home, and secure job, I felt myself slipping down a gradual slope into a land of despair and hopelessness. If something didn't change, I would not survive.

Pain. I had to get away from the pain.

At the prompting of a good friend, I sought career counseling. My job profile had changed over the last several years to the point where I felt like a square peg being jammed into a round hole. It didn't fit, and I was wearing out in the process. Eventually, this stress affected the most important areas of my life—my relationship with my wife and children became painfully strained and began to disintegrate.

I longed for greener pastures.

As part of the counselor's recommended plan, I took a graduate-level class in the area of my identified strengths at a local university. I was dipping my toe in the waters of change, feeling both excited and apprehensive as I entered the classroom. It had been twenty years. Would I be able to handle the academic challenge? And what if this proved to be the right direction for me? Would my family be willing to support my going back to school full time? After all, in the next few years, three of our children would go off to college.

How would we do it?

Answers to those questions materialized throughout the semester. Although the class was challenging, I knew it was where I belonged. So, after long talks with my wife, much counsel from friends, and a lot of prayer, we made the decision to go for it. I would leave my secure job and enter the world of academia to pursue my doctorate. It would be a long journey, over five years.

I felt my Shepherd telling me that He had greener pastures ahead for me, and I felt hope for the first time in years.

As I look back, I wish I could say that all was bliss from that point on. Yes, there was tremendous relief, but the journey involved a lot of work—restoring our marriage, healing emotionally and mentally, stretching our finances, not to mention handling the academic load. My family was supportive, but there were struggles and sacrifices along the way. Pastures don't become green again overnight. It took a while for us to trudge through the valley.

Seven years ago, I had almost given up hope. But I am no longer that man of yesterday. Physically, emotionally, intellectually, socially, and spiritually, I am restored. Christian friends were part of that process—three men in my small group who listened and prayed, a man at work who helped me confront truth, my pastor who came alongside me, my counselor who redirected my focus back to my Shepherd.

My Shepherd—who led me back to green pastures, who restored my soul, who restored my hope.

ACTION STEP

IN A JOURNAL OR A BLANK SHEET OF PAPER, WRITE A LIST OF NINE THINGS YOU WOULD LOVE TO BE PART OF YOUR FUTURE. NUMBER EACH OF THEM AND THEN WRITE DOWN THE NUMBER "10." NEXT TO THAT, WRITE, "WHATEVER GOD WANTS FOR ME." COMMIT THE LIST TO GOD AND PUT IT IN A SAFE PLACE FOR FUTURE REFERENCE.

PRAYER

I do not know what is next in my life, but God, I trust in Your love and Your promises, and believe in my heart that a bright future awaits me.

SMALL MIRACLES

WHEN LIFE GETS PARTICULARLY TOUGH, KEEP YOUR EYES AND HEART OPEN FOR GOD'S SMALL MIRACLES.

To the true disciple a miracle only manifests the power and love which are silently at work everywhere as divinely in the gift of daily bread as in the miraculous multiplication of the loaves.

FREDERICK WILLIAM ROBERTSON

TO THINK ABOUT

- Have you ever experienced an incredible moment when you just knew God was doing something special just for you?
- Do you believe in miracles and divine intervention in your life?
- Do you go throughout your day with a sense of God's love for you?

LESSON FOR LIFE

PROMISES

God will...

Give you rest
Matthew 11:29

Keep His promises
1 Chronicles 16:15

Take care of you
Psalm 37:5

Tender Mercies

BIBLE STUDY PASSAGE: JEREMIAH 31:1-20

Let us, then, feel very sure that we can come before God's throne where there is grace. There we can receive mercy and grace to help us when we need it.

HEBREWS 4:16

When we get to the end of our own strength, realizing that we need God to make it in life and keep our soul tender and true, it's good to remember—

- *God sent a rainbow to Noah as a symbol that His love for man would never waver (Genesis 9:14-15).*
- *God spoke to Moses in a burning bush (Exodus 3:2-6) and parted the waters of the sea with His breath to provide deliverance (Exodus 14:21).*
- *God allowed a young shepherd boy to conquer a mighty warrior with only a sling shot and a single stone (1 Samuel 17:49).*
- *Jesus healed a blind man (Mark 8:22-25), a person with leprosy (Matthew 8:2-3), a man who had never walked (Matthew 9:2-7),*

and even raised a young girl from death to life (Luke 8:51-55).
· *The Holy Spirit came upon the followers of Jesus so they could proclaim God's love in languages they'd never spoken before (Acts 2:4-8).*

God is at work in our world—and in your life. Sometimes all we need is to open our eyes to see His tender mercies in our lives.

Your Father knows the things you need before you ask him.

Matthew 6:8

REAL LIFE

The Heaven-Sent Cross

JULIE PRICE AS TOLD TO CHRISTY PHILIPPE

I stood in front of a conference room full of hotel workers. I always felt confident teaching these seminars. In fact, my work provided me with stability in a turbulent period in my life. At age thirty-two, I was on my own for the first time.

When I dismissed the class for a break, Jim, my boss, steered me into the lobby. There he informed me that the police had contacted my office to let me know that my house had been burglarized.

As I headed to my hotel room to pack, I felt a growing sense of violation—and fear. Sure, I had put up a strong front after Steve left me. But inside I knew I'd only been trying to convince myself that I could take care of myself and live on my own.

On the flight home, I couldn't stop thinking about what the thieves might have taken. The jewelry box on my dresser held a snapshot of my mother as a young girl—and the gold cross that my grandmother had presented to me when I was a year old. That necklace had always made me feel loved and cherished.

When I arrived, I was glad I'd asked my friend Melissa to come with me. The sight of my splintered front door behind the crisscrossed yellow crime scene tape nearly floored me.

The inside was even worse than I had pictured. Everything had been overturned, my precious possessions scattered haphazardly on the floor.

Then it struck me. "My jewelry box—" It was gone.

I spent that night at Melissa's. The next morning, per the policeman's advice, I numbly went to the hardware store for a new door—the sturdiest one I could find. The cashier asked brightly, "Is your husband going to install it?"

I just nodded. What was the use of explaining? *I'll do it myself,* I thought. I *do everything else for myself these days.*

At home, I studied the instructions. *Wow, I can do this,* I thought. Once I got the hinges on, it was time to cut a hole for the doorknob. I made the measurements and carefully began cutting. Almost immediately, I heard the tortured sound of wood splitting. With one slip, I had ruined everything.

I sat on the ground in defeat as tears spilled down my face, turning the sawdust into pulp. *Lord,* I prayed, *I obviously can't take care of myself. Why aren't You helping me?* I thought God was supposed to stay close to me, but I felt abandoned, vulnerable, and alone.

I was angrily stuffing the mess I'd made into the trashcan when, directly at my feet, something gold glinted—my cross!

I picked up the delicate necklace and held it in my palm. It must have fallen out of my jewelry box as the burglars ran off. But there was nothing accidental about it—I had never needed my cross the way I needed it at that moment. "Thank You, Lord," I whispered tearfully. "I am sorry for doubting You. You never turn your back on any of Your children. With You, I am never alone."

I put the cross around my neck and called the hardware store to arrange to have someone come and install a new door. An incredibly reassuring sense of security enveloped me. I would stay in my own bed that night, safe in the certain knowledge that the Lord was watching over me—an assurance that wouldn't be stolen from me again.

ACTION STEP

ONE OF THE KEY WORDS IN THE BIBLE IS "REMEMBER." WE ARE TO REMEMBER GOD'S WORKS, HIS MERCY, HIS FAITHFULNESS. SOMETIMES WE FORGET ALL GOD HAS DONE FOR US. FIND SOME TIME TO WRITE DOWN—

- WHAT YOUR LIFE WAS LIKE BEFORE YOU ENCOUNTERED GOD.
- WHAT GOD DID TO DELIVER YOU FROM "SLAVERY" IN YOUR LIFE.
- THE GRACIOUS DEEDS THE LORD HAS DONE FOR YOU SINCE YOU'VE BEEN WALKING WITH HIM.

TUCK YOUR "STORY" INTO YOUR BIBLE, AND LOOK AT IT AGAIN FROM TIME TO TIME. THIS MIGHT ALSO BE A GREAT TIME TO START A SPIRITUAL JOURNAL IF YOU HAVEN'T ALREADY DONE SO—A DAY-TO-DAY RECORD OF YOUR LIFE WITH GOD.

PRAYER

Dear Heavenly Father, thank You that being Your child means seeing Your comfort and provision in every detail of my life. Thank You for Your goodness.

RECONCILIATION

WITH GOD'S GRACE, EVEN THE MOST DAMAGED RELATIONSHIPS CAN BE RESTORED.

Blessed to us is the night,
for it reveals the stars.

ANONYMOUS

TO THINK ABOUT

- Is there someone in your life from whom you are estranged?
- What is the hardest part of healing a broken relationship?
- Are there some relationships that can never be restored?

PROMISES

God will...

Heal and restore
Isaiah 61:3

Turn enemies into friends
Isaiah 11:6

Bless peacemakers
Matthew 5:9

Redeem your tears
Psalm 126:5

Remove your sorrows
Zephaniah 3:18

Bring justice and
preserve the broken
Isaiah 42:3

Messengers of Peace

BIBLE STUDY PASSAGE: EPHESIANS 2:14-22

In Christ, there is no difference between Jew and Greek, slave and free person, male and female. You are all the same in Christ Jesus.

GALATIANS 3:28

Jesus tells His disciples: "If you forgive anyone his sins, they are forgiven. If you don't forgive them, they are not forgiven" (John 20:23). In the Lord's Prayer, He teaches us: "Forgive us for our sins, just as we have forgiven those who sinned against us" (Matthew 6:12).

One of the most important "soul matters" in God's eyes is reconciliation. Just as He sent His Son Jesus into the world to reconcile people to Him (Colossians 1:20-22), so He gives us the mandate to be peacemakers, to be reconciled even to our enemies (Matthew 5:44).

But my husband left me. My friend betrayed me. I can't trust my boss.

Obviously, one person cannot control or force the process of reconciliation. That's why we are told to keep peace "as

162

much as depends on you" (Romans 12:18 NKJV). But before ignoring the call to reconciliation as too hard, too painful, and very unrealistic, we need to remember—

He does everything just
right and on time.
Ecclesiastes 3:11

- *Reconciliation is God's idea and His way of doing things (Romans 5:8-10).*
- *Reconciliation is tied to our worship of God—He wants us to come before Him with right relationships (Matthew 5:23).*
- *As we forgive others, we are forgiven by God (Luke 6:37).*
- *One of the blessings of walking with God is peace (Galatians 5:22).*

A few notes of caution on this topic include—

- *Reconciliation does not always happen all at once, but can take place over years, so don't get discouraged or give up by lack of results (Galatians 6:9).*
- *Reconciliation does not mean we submit ourselves to abuse and the cruelty and lack of response of others. Even Jesus told His disciples to avoid certain people (Matthew 10:14).*
- *Reconciliation cannot always be made completely manifest due to past sins. Someone who has left a spouse and family may seek forgiveness, but not necessarily be able to reenter the lives of those whom they left in the same way.*

REAL LIFE

Years of the Locusts

NANETTE THORSEN-SNIPES

The shock of learning I had another grandchild was too much. I broke down in tears—tears of joy, mixed with grief because of lost years. My new grandchild wasn't a baby wrapped in a cuddly blue blanket. He was thirteen and stood half a head taller than me.

Years before, I knew there was a possibility that he was part of my family, but I never knew for sure. Even so, I prayed for him. As the years passed, I thought of him less often—until the day my son walked into the kitchen and announced he had another child. Tears streamed down my face at the thought of all the wasted years—years the locusts had eaten. How I wanted to know this child who grew up without a father and whose mother still struggled to provide. I began that day to pray not only for my son and his wife, but also for my new grandson and his mother.

Within a month, I finally met him. My heart leapt when I saw his father's features mirrored in his face. He had dark brown hair and blue eyes that seemed to say, "It's good to be home." Without hesitation, I hugged him close—this child who looked so much like the rest of us.

The first few weeks of getting to know my grandson were awkward. I felt like a gangly teenager trying to start a new relationship. One evening, with the encouragement of friends, my husband and I invited him to a Christian concert at a nearby church.

I could barely contain my joy standing beside this newest family member and watching the on-stage singer rouse the auditorium with praise. I clapped to the music, and oh so gradually, my grandson started to clap, too.

At one point, the singer stopped and spoke about Jesus. He said, "Some of us don't know our fathers, but we know that God loves us anyway, and we can always count on Him, our Abba, Father." He pointed heavenward.

I tried to stop the tears, but they slid down my cheeks. I squeezed my grandson's hand, trying to let him know that I felt his pain at being left without a father for so long. I prayed he would squeeze my hand, too, so I knew he understood, but he didn't.

Another week slipped by before I saw him again. This time he ate supper with us and we watched a video. After the movie, my husband volunteered to take him home while I tidied up the house and got ready for bed. As always, I wondered how my grandchild felt about me and prayed it wasn't too late to develop a relationship.

When my husband returned, I asked how everything went. He said they had sat in the front seat talking about hunting, fishing, and other things for a few moments. When my grandson got out, the last thing he said was, "Tell Grandma I love her."

ACTION STEP

WHO IS SOMEONE WITH WHOM YOU ARE SEPARATED DUE TO A MAJOR OR MINOR GRIEVANCE? HOW SERIOUS IS THE CAUSE OF THE SEPARATION? WHAT MAKES IT HARDEST FOR YOU TO SEEK RAPPROCHEMENT? WHAT IS ONE SMALL STEP YOU CAN TAKE TODAY? ARE YOU READY?

PRAYER

Thank You, O God, that when I was far away from You and lost, You ventured to seek me out. Grant me the courage to be a peacemaker in my world.

HOPE

HOPE IS WHEN WE TRUST OUR FUTURE INTO GOD'S HANDS, EVEN WHEN THINGS ARE LESS THAN IDEAL IN THE PRESENT.

Hope is some extraordinary spiritual grace
that God gives us to control our fears, not to oust them.
VINCENT MCNABB

TO THINK ABOUT

- If we lost all sense of hope, how would our world spin out of control?
- Have you ever had your hope rekindled during a difficult time of discouragement?
- How can you encourage a sense of hope in others?

 LESSON FOR LIFE

PROMISES

God will...

Give you hope through
Scripture
Romans 15:4

Keep His promises
Hebrews 6:18

Provide everything you
need
Psalm 130:7

Reasons to Hope

BIBLE STUDY PASSAGE: ROMANS 5:1-5

Be joyful because you have hope. Be patient when trouble comes, and pray at all times.

ROMANS 12:12

When a man named Saul met Jesus Christ in a blinding light, his life was never the same. He went from persecutor to encourager; from arrogant braggart to humble preacher; from self-sufficient to reliant on God. One other remarkable change that took place in Paul's life is that instead of keeping his eyes on the past, he now looked to the future with an incredible sense of hope (Philippians 3:13-14).

Some reasons that Paul says we can live with hope even in the midst of adversity include—

- *God forgives us—"Since we have been made right with God by our faith, we have peace with God" (Romans 5:1). When we are at peace with our Creator, the future is always bright.*
- *God favors us—"But God shows his great love for us in this way: Christ died for us while we were still sinners" (Romans*

168

5:8).   We don't have to crawl to God and beg Him to help us with our problems.   He is absolutely crazy about you.   He loved you even when you rebelled against Him.

- *God turns suffering into hope—"We also have joy with our troubles, because we know that these troubles produce patience.   And patience produces character, and character produces hope" (Romans 5:3-4).   With God at work in our lives, the very trials that could crush our spirits actually make our hope even stronger.*

- *God helps us when we are weak—"When we were unable to help ourselves, at the moment of our need, Christ died for us, although we were living against God" (Romans 5:6).   One of the reasons we feel hopeless is that we just don't believe we have what it takes to overcome challenges.   Not to worry, says God: I'll do for you what you can't do for yourself.*

Hope keeps us youthful, optimistic, and joyful.   Turn to your Heavenly Father today to rekindle that flame in your soul.

These things encourage us who came to God for safety.   They give us strength to hold on to the hope we have been given.   We have this hope as an anchor for the soul, sure and strong.
Hebrews 6:18 19

The Yellow Bird

KAREN MAJORIS-GARRISON

Hope sometimes visits us in different shapes and sizes.   On an autumn day in October, it came to a young couple from our church in the form of a yellow bird.

Scott and Janice had tried for many years to have a baby, and when their son, Scotty, entered the world, the church celebrated right along with them. Soon, however, the doctors diagnosed Scotty with serious heart problems.

Rallying behind the young family, our church supported and reminded them of God's promise never to fail or forsake His children.   Nine months passed, and Scotty's doctors determined that he needed open-heart surgery. His chances of surviving the operation were slim, but, without it, his chances of living past his first birthday were slimmer.

Throughout his ordeal, one thing had become amazingly clear about Scotty: He absolutely loved the color yellow.   Whenever he caught a glimpse of the bright hue anywhere, he squealed in delight.   Even his nurses added a touch of yellow to their uniforms when caring for him.

Sadly, Scotty's operation was not successful.   The attempt to save his little heart failed.

His parents, grief-stricken, escaped to a friend's vacation home soon after the funeral.   Weeks passed, but the gaping wound left by Scotty's absence remained unbearable. One sunset evening, Scotty's parents walked along the beach. Once a threesome, they now clutched each other's hands with the dark realization that Scotty's tiny fingers would never again be clasped between theirs. Too heavy a cross to bear, their grief left them feeling completely desolate and alone, until a reminder of hope expelled the darkness.

It appeared in the form of a bright yellow bird that had landed between them as they walked along the water's edge. Neither parent had ever seen such a bird before nor, unbelievably, had it scurried or flown away, but continued to scamper between them on their barefoot journey in the sand.

Soon, the bird's comforting presence filled them with peace the peace granted to believers in 1 Thessalonians 4:13-14: "Brothers and sisters, we want you to know about those Christians who have died so you will not be sad, as others who have no hope. We believe that Jesus died and that he rose again. So, because of him, God will raise with Jesus those who have died."

After they'd made it back to their beachfront house, the bird remained, studying them for a few moments before lifting its wings and heading towards the sky.

While watching its graceful flight, they imagined Scotty, in the presence of God, soaring high above the clouds and making his way to that incredible yellow ball for a warm kiss upon his chubby cheek.

Today, Scott and Janice's tragic cross to bear is made lighter by the trust that carries it. When questions of why plague them, they can be reminded of God's faithfulness to walk beside them and His willingness to lift them when they fall.

After all, hope had come to them. It appeared in the form of a yellow bird—a gentle messenger fashioned by the Creator's own hands, and carrying with it seeds of comfort, promise, and sunshiny love.

ACTION STEP

PLANTS, FLOWERS, TREES, AND OTHER VEGETATION LAY DORMANT IN DARK SOIL FOR A SEASON, ONLY TO MIRACULOUSLY BREAK FORTH IN LIFE. HOPE IS THE SAME WAY.

STOP BY A NURSERY AND PURCHASE A SEED PACKET OR SMALL PLANT OF A FLOWER OR VEGETABLE YOU LOVE. PLANT THE SEED AND CARE FOR IT. KEEP THE POT ON A WINDOWSILL YOU PASS OFTEN AS A BRIGHT REMINDER THAT HOPE IS NEVER LOST.

PRAYER

Father God, You know the things I'm facing today that threaten to suffocate my hope. Thank You for the goodness and mercy that rekindle hope in my heart. Help me, God, to share that hope with others.

BLESSING OTHERS

WHEN WE JOYFULLY RECEIVE GOD'S BLESSINGS, THE JOY SPILLS OVER AND BLESSES OTHERS.

God's gifts put man's best dreams to shame.

ELIZABETH BARRETT BROWNING

 TO THINK ABOUT

- When have you been blessed by another person's joy?
- Have you blessed others because of your joyful love for God?
- What are some specific ways you can share God's joy with others more often?

LESSON FOR LIFE

PROMISES

God will...

Hear your prayers
Psalm 4:3

Show you mercy and
kindness
Psalm 103:17-18

Bless you and give you
peace
Numbers 6:24-26

Help you during hard
times
Isaiah 43:2-3

My Cup Runneth Over

BIBLE STUDY PASSAGE: 2 CORINTHIANS 9:6-11

I taught you to remember the words Jesus said: "It is more blessed to give than to receive."

ACTS 20:35

One of the greatest—but most neglected—sources of joy and blessings in one's life is through bringing joy and blessing to others.   Despite the various psychological and sociological studies that prove the happiest people in the world are those who serve others, volunteerism in America and throughout the world is at an all-time low.

No question, life is filled to the brim with work, priorities, and pressures that can tap our strength, but perhaps if we reached out more, we would discover more energy and joy than we knew was possible.

Jesus taught His disciples that it is more blessed to give than to receive.   One obvious—but easily forgotten—reason is that if you are giving to others, it implies you have something to give in the first place!   Most of us can count many blessings in our lives right now.   But can we just as easily count the number of ways that we bless others?

In Deuteronomy 16, the children of Israel are reminded to come before the Lord to worship. Three yearly feasts had been established as special times to grow closer to God. Passover, the subject of chapter 16, was to be celebrated at the beginning of the year to commemorate that God had delivered Israel from oppression and slavery (Exodus 12:2). What a blessing! One of the clear expectations when the people attended the feast was spelled out in our study verse, 16:17: As God has blessed you, bring a gift of gratitude to bless God and others. Everyone is not asked to bring the same or an equal gift, but only according to what God has given them.

Have you been blessed? Has God answered your prayers? It is wonderful to serve a God who wants to bless you, but let's not forget to bless others in equal measure.

Each of you must bring a gift that will show how much the Lord your God has blessed you.

Deuteronomy 16:17

REAL LIFE

Twice Blessed

KATHRYN LAY

We knew the call would come eventually, but we weren't sure when. And then it came.

For ten years, Richard and I had prayed that we'd become parents. After a false pregnancy and lost dreams, God showed us that hope was not lost as we were accepted into an adoption program.

We spent six months taking parenting classes, filling out paperwork, and agonizing over home visits from our caseworker. When everything was completed and we were approved, months went by where we were considered for one child or another, but always passed over for someone else. Somehow, I believe God had a very special child in mind for us.

Nine months after we began classes—an ironic duration in God's joyous ways—the call we'd waited for came.

"Her name is Michelle," our caseworker said. On that day, we learned of our imminent adoption of our nine-month-old daughter. And her birthname was the name we'd chosen for our first child twelve years earlier before we were married.

It was time to celebrate. As promised, we called our closest friends and treated them to a special celebration dinner.

While we laughed and talked at the restaurant, telling them of what we knew about our soon-to-arrive and much prayed-for daughter, I became aware that the older couple in the booth behind us laughed as we did and nodded knowingly as we voiced our excitement and nervousness.

We weren't quiet. We were full of joy at the good news. It bubbled over as we talked and planned in the restaurant.

"What if we're not good parents?" I asked.

"What if the adoption doesn't go through and we lose her after we've fallen in love?" Richard asked.

"I bet she's sweet and adorable and full of smiles," I said.

"I bet she'll be a daddy's girl," Richard said.

The louder we got, the more I noticed how quiet the older couple became. But I was too excited to worry, too scared to stop talking.

When the couple behind us left their booth, they paused at our table.

"Congratulations," the woman said, patting my shoulder.

"Thank you," I said, grateful that they weren't angry at our loudness.

She leaned closer. "We have a granddaughter that was adopted by a couple not long ago. I've never seen her. Hearing your excitement, I feel in my heart that somewhere she is loved and well taken care of by a family like you."

Patting my shoulder once more, she whispered, "I'll pray for you and your baby."

At a time when we were blessed and overflowing with joy, God put us in a place where we could be a blessing and comfort to another. I prayed for that grand-mother, that God gave her peace and comfort for the grand-daughter she wondered about. And I knew that my husband and I were in her prayers that night.

ACTION STEP

WHAT IS AN UNMET NEED IN YOUR CHURCH, YOUR NEIGHBORHOOD, YOUR COMMUNITY? TAKE TIME THIS WEEK TO PRAYERFULLY CONSIDER ONE WAY THAT GOD HAS BLESSED YOU SO THAT YOU ARE BETTER PREPARED TO BLESS OTHERS.

PRAYER

Thank You, Heavenly Father, for the many ways You have met my needs and bless me so richly. Give me a joyful gratitude that spills those blessings into the lives of others.

LIFE'S STORMS

WHEN LIFE IS DIFFICULT, WE COME OUT VICTORIOUS THROUGH FAITH, COURAGE, PERSEVERANCE—AND JOY.

When you get into a tight place and everything goes against you, till it seems as though you could not hang on a minute longer, never give up then, for that is just the place and time that the tide will turn.

HARRIET BEECHER STOWE

 TO THINK ABOUT

- Have there been times in your life that you wanted to "throw in the towel" rather than keep going?
- Have you ever given up when things got difficult? What happened?
- What storm in your life are you waiting out right now?

LESSON FOR LIFE

PROMISES

God will...

Enable you to overcome
Habakkuk 3:19

Give you strength and
boldness
Psalm 138:3

Equip you for good works
2 Thessalonians 2:16-17

Never leave you
John 14:18

Joy in a Jail Cell

BIBLE STUDY PASSAGE: PHILIPPIANS 4:10-19

I press toward the goal for the prize of the upward call of God in Christ Jesus.

PHILIPPIANS 3:14 NKJV

Philippians is known as a book about joy—some form of the word appears in nine verses in this relatively short letter—despite being written by Paul from a Roman prison. In both his words and his actions, Paul calls for us to rejoice, to be joyful, in spite of suffering (ch. 1), in the midst of humble service (ch. 2), and in the face of fear and anxiety (ch. 4).

But is it practical to think we can rejoice in any situation? In the face of a terminal illness? When we face financial woes? When one of our children is struggling morally and spiritually? Is it even healthy to find joy in such times?

Note that Paul does not say rejoice because of hardship; he says rejoice despite and in the midst of pain. Paul doesn't call us to be masochists who wish for hardship and pain in our lives, but he does call us to be overcomers in all circumstances.

And Paul knows what he's talking about. This is the man

who was stoned and beaten (Acts 14:19, 21:30-32), ship-wrecked (Acts 27:39), suffered from a painful physical ailment (Galatians 4:13-14), lived with the guilt of being a persecutor of innocent people in his past (Acts 22:4), and was imprisoned and sentenced to death for his faith (Acts 16:22-24). But like the Energizer Bunny, he just kept on going and going and going. Why? How? He was a man of joy.

Paul's final message to the Philippians concerns the way this church cared for him in the midst of his trials. He says that their gifts and compassion were "a sweet-smelling sacrifice offered to God, who accepts that sacrifice and is pleased with it" (4:18). Helping someone else persevere is a fragrant, pleasing prayer to God!

Yes, life can be difficult. But even in the midst of suffering we can stand firm—and help others to do the same—as we find our ultimate joy in the Lord.

May our Lord Jesus Christ himself and God our Father encourage you and strengthen you in every good thing you do and say. God loved us, and through his grace he gave us a good hope and encouragement that continues forever.
2 Thessalonians 2:16-17

REAL LIFE

Heroes Among Us

MELINDA LANCASTER

A few days ago, I saw one—a hero, I mean.   It wasn't at the movie theater or on a television screen.   He wore no "S" on his shirt, no cape on his back, but his bravery was still very visible to me.   He was not tall, dark, and handsome as the world portrays all heroes to be.   He didn't fly or disappear and didn't seem aware of his "hero status."   Nevertheless, he is indeed a hero and certainly thought very brave by those who love him.

Entering the elevator at the hospital, I noticed a little boy next to me. Immediately I recognized the fuzzy hair just growing out from what was probably his last bout with chemotherapy.   It looked like he had won some battles, but still had yet to win the war.

As the mother of a son, my heart was immediately drawn to him.   Quietly I watched him and noticed a cell phone next to his ear.   He was softly crying, and the tear stains on his cheeks showed he had been weeping for awhile.   I heard what sounded like a male voice on the other end of the phone.   Though I couldn't hear the conversation, this little one repeated the same words over and over, "Because I don't feel good."

I gathered his daddy was asking him why he was crying.   His words pierced my heart.   Most would be in their mother's arms being cradled closely.   Not this little hero.   Though his tears were telling a story, he stood very proud and tough.

That's what happens when you look death straight in the eyes, or when you have endured more pain than most will suffer their whole lives. That's what happens when you keep fighting though the odds are against you and when the struggle for life is greater than the power of death.

Suddenly, my problems looked microscopic. What I have gone through along with what I have yet to experience would probably not equal what this little one has suffered. Though his face will probably never make it to the six o'clock news or the front of a cereal box, it will never leave my mind. God let me see him at that moment for a reason: He wanted his plight to rescue me from my pain and disappointments and, perhaps, even my despair. He succeeded—just as any true "superman" would.

In his words of encouragement to his dad (yes, he was telling his dad that everything was going to be all right)—sprinkled with both tears and laughter— was a mountain of courage, the strength of a giant, and the heart of a lion. In his smile he showed his refusal to give up the fight.

Sometimes we look for heroes in all the wrong places. Let Jesus be your heavenly Hero, but look for inspiration in places you least expect to find it, like in the strong fighting stance of a very sick but joyful little boy on an elevator in the middle of the afternoon.

ACTION STEP

ONE OF THE BEST WAYS WE CAN GROW IN COMPASSION IS THROUGH SIMPLE ACTS OF KINDNESS.   LOOK INTO SPENDING A MORNING OR AFTERNOON IN VOLUNTEER SERVICE AT A LOCAL HOSPITAL, THE SALVATION ARMY, OR ANOTHER COMPASSIONATE MINISTRY IN YOUR HOMETOWN.

PRAYER

When I am tossed in the winds and waves of life's storms, grant me a calm, confident, joyful heart that stands strong against all trials.

SHARING LIFE

DEEP IN OUR SOULS, WE ALL NEED THE ENCOURAGEMENT AND SUPPORT OF OTHERS.

The friend who can be silent with us in a moment of despair or confusion, who can stay with us in an hour of grief and bereavement, who can tolerate not knowing, not curing, not healing and face with us the reality of our powerlessness, that is a friend who cares.

HENRI NOUWEN

 To Think About

- Are you comfortable sharing personal areas of concern and need with others?
- Why are we so often tempted to try to handle life without the support and encouragement of others?
- How have you been able to encourage others to grow in their walk with Christ?

LESSON FOR LIFE

PROMISES

God will...

Be pleased with your
love for your neighbor
Romans 13:8

Reproduce His love in
you
1 John 4:19

Hear your prayers as you
pray for each other
James 5:16

Unify His church
John 17:21

We Really Do Need Each Other!

BIBLE STUDY PASSAGE: GALATIANS 6:1-9

If one falls down, the other can help him up. But it is bad for the person who is alone and falls, because no one is there to help.

ECCLESIASTES 4:10

In the sixth chapter of Galatians, Paul sets out some of the most practical principles for expressing love for one another found anywhere in the Bible. But just because they are practical doesn't make them easy!

First, he tells us that we should be redemptive people, helping restore those who have been caught in a sin (v. 1). He does caution you that as you reach out to help someone, be extra careful not to get trapped in sin yourself.

Second, Paul challenges us to love others unconditionally, without judgment and comparisons (v. 4). Competition can be friendly and healthy, but when it consumes our relationships, the inevitable result is conflict. How many marital and sibling relationships have been torpedoed by a spirit of striving rather than a spirit of pulling together?

Next, Paul urges us to help carry the "excessive weights" that others are forced to bear (v. 2). He does point out that each of us should carry our own "backpacks," so we aren't required to do everything for others (v. 5). But when someone has burdens that are bigger than any one person should handle alone, we are to step in help.

Most importantly, Paul reminds us not to give up on loving others (v. 9). Sure, some people are difficult to love, but if we don't lose faith in God's power to authentically change their lives, our steadfast persistence may be the very thing that makes the difference between them finding God's forgiveness and peace or never receiving God's grace in their hearts.

The result of how we relate to others is simple, according to Paul. He says, "People harvest only what they plant" (v. 7). When we sow love into others, we will ultimately receive love in return. And the truth is that we all need that kind of love for a healthy soul.

If two or three people come together in my name, I am there with them.

Matthew 18:20

REAL LIFE

Something Special in the Dining Room

JOANNE SCHULTE

I could never have imagined how special my luncheon would turn out to be, but I knew it would be different from all I had hosted previously, and I wondered why.

Each of the "young at heart" senior ladies on the guest list thanked me for her invitation and said how much she was looking forward to the day. Although I often entertain, for some reason I was anticipating this event more than most.

When the guests arrived, my house was sparkling clean, and everything about it said, "Welcome." Beautiful china and home grown flowers adorned the table while food waited in the kitchen for the perfect moment to be served.

The chatter of the ladies filled my dining room like a ray of sunshine. Sometimes I would interject a question or comment, but mostly I basked in the pleasure of listening to them talk—getting to know them better in the process. I wondered why I had waited so long to have this luncheon.

Because they were good friends, my guests felt free to talk about the physical and emotional pains they were experiencing, and I realized their beautiful, smiling faces masked hurting hearts and bodies. However, this was not a pity party I was witnessing, but a sharing of common experiences, a bonding of lives. From time to time heads nodded as if to say, "I understand." And now and then someone would use her handkerchief to wipe away a tear. It would have been difficult to say anything with the lump in my throat, but nothing needed to be said just now.

After a long pause, one woman bowed her head and prayed out loud for the cares and concerns that had just been expressed. She prayed for only a few moments, but what a difference those few moments made. Time was suspended. Eyes did not open nor did heads look up right away. No one spoke for quite a while, but the looks on their faces said their problems already seemed easier to handle. Their eyes were full of thankfulness and hope. It had been a special moment.

They seemed hesitant to leave, but as they did, each lady hugged me and thanked me—expressing once again just how much she had enjoyed the luncheon.

After I said good-bye to the last guest, I deliberately paused to let the warm glow from the luncheon linger in my thoughts. I doubted any luncheon could ever surpass this one. Those lovely ladies had been my guests. But because I enjoyed them so much, I had the strangest feeling I had been their guest for something special in the dining room—along with Someone very special indeed.

ACTION STEP

ARE THERE ONE OR TWO PEOPLE CLOSE TO YOU AT CHURCH WHOSE BURDENS YOU CAN STEP UP TO CARRY? OR IS THERE A NEED IN YOUR LIFE YOU NEED TO SHARE WITH SOMEONE ELSE? TAKE A STEP TODAY—MAKE A PHONE CALL OR SEND AN E-MAIL TO OFFER PRAYERS OR REQUEST PRAYERS, OR BOTH. THEN WRITE ON YOUR CALENDAR OR IN YOUR PALM ONE THING YOU CAN DO TO HELP THAT PERSON OR THOSE PEOPLE WITH THE THINGS THEY'RE FACING.

PRAYER

God, thank You that You didn't create us to live in isolation, but to help each other seek and find You. Show me who to reach out to today.

ATTITUDE

THE QUALITY OF OUR LIFE IS MORE DEPENDENT ON OUR PERSPECTIVE THAN OUR CIRCUMSTANCES.

A loving person lives in a loving world. A hostile person lives in a hostile world; everyone you meet is your mirror.

KEN KEYES, JR.

 TO THINK ABOUT

- How do you feel when you are around someone who has a consistently negative, critical, cynical attitude? Do you ever notice?
- Are there some negative attitude issues in your life? How would you like to improve your attitude? What are some strengths you can build on?

PROMISES

God will...

Renew your mind
Hebrews 8:10

Perfect your character
through patience
James 1:4

Give you patience and
renew your soul
2 Corinthians 4:16

Give you peace and rest
Isaiah 26:3

Hallmarks of a Great Attitude

BIBLE STUDY PASSAGE: PHILIPPIANS 2:3-11

Do not be interested only in your own life, but be interested in the lives of others.

PHILIPPIANS 2:4

Have you ever had a stinky enough attitude that you didn't even want to be around yourself? A negative, critical, harsh attitude is poison to relationships—and to your soul.

If you're suffering from a bad case of negativity, here are some sure-fire cures to get your thoughts and perspective moving in the right direction—

- *Smile: "Be full of joy in the Lord always. I will say again, be full of joy" (Philippians 4:4). Our countenance is often a reflection of what we're feeling inside. Even if you don't feel happy inside, fake it until you feel it.*
- *Say "thank you" often: "Let the peace that Christ gives control your thinking, because you were all called together in one body to have peace. Always be thankful" (Colossians 3:15). When we take others for granted and see only their faults, our attitude*

192

toward them—and theirs toward us—will go downhill fast. Express appreciation.

- *Forgive fast:* "Do not let the sun go down on your wrath" (Ephesians 4:26 NKJV). Unresolved anger and grudges cause us to hurt others—and ourselves. Even if you have to swallow your pride and do all the hard work, work things out right now. Jesus says don't even go to church without clearing things up with your brother (Matthew 5:23-25).
- *Be proactive:* "Let us think about each other and help each other to show love and do good deeds" (Hebrews 10:24). Instead of moaning and groaning and complaining about how bad things are, act. Inaction is a breeding ground for negativity.
- *Watch your words:* "When you talk, do not say harmful things, but say what people need" (Ephesians 4:29). What we say has a tremendous impact on how we feel. Do your words make you more or less positive?
- *Cheer up someone else:* "By helping each other with your troubles, you truly obey the law of Christ" (Galatians 6:2). If you're feeling sorry for yourself, find someone who really has problems, and help them see life through the eyes of faith and hope again. It will help you, too.

Rejoice. Your new attitude begins today!

In your lives you must think and act like Christ Jesus.
Philippians 2:5

193

REAL LIFE

Love is the Answer

NANETTE THORSEN-SNIPES

My day began on a sour note when I saw my six-year-old wrestling with a limb of my azalea bush.   By the time I got outside, he'd broken it.

"Can I take this to school today?" he asked.

With a wave of my hand, I sent him on.   I turned my back so he wouldn't see the tears.   I touched the limb of my favorite bush as if to say, *I'm sorry.*

I wished I could have said that to my husband earlier, but I'd been angry. The washing machine had leaked on my linoleum.   *If Jim had just taken the time to fix it the night before....*   I tossed my husband's dishes into sudsy water.

Later, I lugged wet clothes to the Laundromat.   Thinking how love had gone out of my life, I stared at wall graffiti, feeling as wrung-out as clothes in a washer.   I hung up shirts, then left for school to pick up my son.

I knocked on the classroom door and his teacher motioned for me to wait. She whispered something to Jonathan and gave him crayons.

"I want to talk to you about Jonathan," she said when she walked over to me.

I steeled myself for the worst.   I had had a fight with Jim, my son had broken a limb off my favorite bush, and now this.

"Did you know Jonathan brought flowers to school today?"

I nodded, trying to keep tears in check.   I glanced at my son coloring a picture.   His hair flopped beneath his brow.   He brushed it away and grinned at his handiwork.

"See that little girl?" the teacher asked.

Watching a bright-eyed child laugh out loud, I nodded.

"Yesterday she was hysterical.   Her parents are going through a divorce. She said she wished she could die.   I watched her bury her face in her hands and say, 'Nobody loves me.'   I did all I could to console her, but—"

"I thought you wanted to talk to me about Jonathan."

"I do."   She touched my arm lightly.   "Today your son walked over to that child, and handed her some pretty pink flowers.   Then he whispered, 'I love you.'"

My heart swelled with pride for what Jonathan did.   I reached for his hand, and said to his teacher, "You've made my day!"

Later that evening, I pulled weeds from around my lopsided azalea bush. My mind wandered back to the love Jonathan showed the little girl and a biblical verse came to mind: "Now these three remain: faith, hope and love. But the greatest of these is love."   My son had practiced love, but all day I had only thought of how angry I was with Jim.

I heard the familiar squeak of Jim's truck brakes as he pulled into the drive, and I snapped a small limb bristling with hot pink azaleas.   I felt the seed of love God planted in my family beginning to bloom once again in me.

My husband's eyes widened in surprise as I handed him the flowers.   "I love you," I said.

ACTION STEP

ATTITUDE IS SO FOUNDATIONAL TO THE QUALITY OF LIFE WE LIVE THAT MAYBE WE NEED TO GET BACK TO BASICS. BEFORE YOU LAUGH THIS ACTIVITY OFF AS TOO SIMPLE, ASK YOURSELF: HOW BAD DO I NEED A BETTER ATTITUDE?

GO TO A CRAFT STORE OR THE SCHOOL SUPPLIES SECTION OF ANOTHER RETAIL OUTLET. BUY NOTECARDS AND STICKERS—ESPECIALLY GOLD STARS. LABEL A NOTECARD FOR EVERY DAY OF THIS COMING WEEK. EVERY TIME YOU EXPRESS A POSITIVE ATTITUDE, ADD A BRIGHT, COLORFUL, HAPPY STICKER TO THE CARD. WHEN YOU EXPRESS A NEGATIVE ATTITUDE, ADHERE A FROWNING FACE OR OTHER SAD STICKER.

AT THE END OF THE WEEK, TAKE A LOOK AND SEE HOW YOU'RE DOING.

PRAYER

Father, You have given me a great life. Help me enjoy the wonderful things You've given me by having a great attitude.

PRIORITIES

NOTHING IN OUR LIVES IS AS IMPORTANT AS SEEKING AND OBEYING GOD.

The things that matter most in this world,
they can never be held in our hands.

GLORIA GAITHER

 TO THINK ABOUT

- Do you feel pressured to be perfect in certain areas of your life? Do you thing God measures your performance the same way you do?
- What are your priorities? Do you think your life reflects those priorities?
- How has God shown you what He thinks is most important for your life?

LESSON FOR LIFE

First Things First

BIBLE STUDY PASSAGE: LUKE 10:38-42

Only one thing is important. Mary has chosen the better thing, and it will never be taken away from her.

LUKE 10:42

In the famous parable of the lost son (Luke 15:11-32), a young man rejects his father's teachings and authority, demands his inheritance, and heads for a distant land where he squanders his financial and moral wealth. The loving father never gives up on this prodigal, and when his young son does come to his senses and ashamedly returns home, he welcomes him with open arms. He honors him with a feast, a party, a special cloak, and a golden ring. The older brother, who has faithfully stood by his father's side this whole time, is enraged that the prodigal should receive such a welcome. The father sadly reminds this older son that you don't have to work in a pig sty like his younger brother did to have a piggy attitude. Both sons learn about forgiveness and reconciliation from the love of their father.

In our study passage, we discover that Martha, much like

the older brother, holds deep resentment toward a younger sibling. No, Mary is not immoral and rebellious, but she certainly doesn't have Martha's sense of responsibility. She leaves the dishes and chores to her sister so that she can sit at Jesus' feet. Wouldn't you feel a little resentful, too?

Jesus' answer to Martha's demand that He tell Mary to get busy is: "Martha, Martha, you are worried and upset about many things. Only one thing is important. Mary has chosen the better thing, and it will never be taken away from her" (vv. 41-42).

Is Jesus' point that we not care for our responsibilities? Of course not. But He does remind us that the heart of our faith, our reason for living, is to love and worship God. Nothing else comes first!

Your heart will be where your treasure is.
Luke 12:34

199

REAL LIFE

This Marine's Wakeup Call

JOE H. STARGEL (LT. COL. JOSEPH H. STARGEL, JR., USMCR RETIRED)

I don't have time for this, I fretted while checking into the hospital that wintry morning. *The City Council meets next week, my Reservist duty weekend is coming up, and my desk at work is piled high.*

Regardless, I followed the doctor's orders and the next day found me in the surgery recovery room, invaded on all sides by needles and tubes, with a twelve-inch vertical incision on my abdomen held together by wire stitches.

The enemy? Reticulum cell sarcoma, a rare cancer of the lymph system. The prognosis? Five percent chance of slowing the fast-multiplying cells. Possibility for a cure? None. Life expectancy? Between six weeks and six months.

I had joined the Marine Corps at seventeen. Years earlier, when I was released from active duty, I plunged into finding work and catching up on schooling. Meantime, Gloria and I married and set about to realize our dream: a family. When our sons Randy and Rick were born, we felt complete.

Somewhere in the process, though, my life got out of kilter. A workaholic and a loner, I devoted more and more time to getting further ahead: a hundred-mile commute for two law degrees, nine years on city commission, two years as mayor, monthly weekend drills as an active Marine reservist, plus a full-time job as corporate counsel with a road construction firm.

My strivings left little time for my family or God. Still, I considered myself a loving husband, good father, acceptable Christian. Didn't I work twelve hours every day to provide for my family? Didn't I go to church most Sunday mornings? Wasn't that enough?

When cancer struck, reality struck as well. My family had changed—Randy now a college junior, Rick a high-school senior, Gloria a wife I hardly knew, and *me* lacking spiritual strength.

I began fighting cancer the only way I knew how: *Stay busy. Don't think. Maybe it'll go away.*

Following that year of debilitating treatments, my oncologist adopted a "wait and see" policy, offering no hope for long-term remission. It was like a time bomb: I bore the ever-present fear that cancer would reactivate at any moment.

My wife, though, became convinced that God wanted to heal me and bombarded heaven's gates on my behalf. Her faith and optimism proved contagious and made me ask, *Just what are my priorities?*

Finally I recognized my illness as one dynamite wakeup call—a heaven-played reveille. "Joe," the message read, "you've had it all backwards. As important and necessary as work is, a truly successful person puts God first, family second, and work last."

Months later, on a typical Sunday afternoon, I joined Gloria in the den. "Honey, are you ready for our walk? We have enough time before church."

Yep. This workaholic heard—and heeded—his wakeup call: *Take time to live.*

ACTION STEP

ARE YOU EXPERIENCING THE JOY OF THE LORD IN YOUR LIFE RIGHT NOW? DOES LOVING GOD COME FIRST? THE NEXT TIME YOU FEEL OVERWHELMED BY THE VARIOUS DEMANDS IN YOUR LIFE, ACT COUNTERINTUITIVELY BY STOPPING RIGHT THAT SECOND AND TAKING A MOMENT TO PRAISE AND WORSHIP YOUR LOVING HEAVENLY FATHER.

PRAYER

Turn my heart and mind to You right now, O God, my kind and gracious Lord. I put You before all other relationships, all other tasks.

INTEGRITY

IT IS VITAL TO OUR SOUL THAT WE PURSUE MORAL EXCELLENCE IN EVERY DETAIL OF OUR LIVES.

A promise must never be broken.

ALEXANDER HAMILTON

 To Think About

- How much integrity do you see on display in our culture? Where you work and live?
- Have you ever compromised on your values and beliefs? How did that make you feel?
- Have you ever suffered negative consequences for keeping your word and doing what you knew was the right thing?

LESSON FOR LIFE

A Clear Conscience

BIBLE STUDY PASSAGE: PSALM 24:1-6

*You must have true and honest weights and measures so
that you will live a long time in the land the Lord your
God is giving you.*

DEUTERONOMY 25:15

All around us, integrity is crumbling. There are too many
examples of dishonesty to ignore this as a huge life issue. So
what does the Bible have to say about integrity?

- *Integrity means treating people fairly and honestly: "The Lord
  wants honest balances and scales" (Proverbs 16:11). Any gain
  from cheating or fudging the truth is sure to be temporary.
  The long-term impact is always a breech of trust.*
- *Integrity is giving your word and keeping it: "Don't say things
  that are false" (Proverbs 24:28). Many of us want to "please"
  the people in our lives and say what they want to hear—only
  to have to backtrack and apologize later. Be direct and honest
  up front—your reputation for follow through is at stake. (See
  Exodus 8:28-32.)*

- *Integrity is more valuable than riches: "Riches gotten by doing wrong have no value, but right living will save you from death" (Proverbs 10:2). True wealth comes from a true character.*
- *Beware of bad influences: "Bad friends will ruin good habits" (1 Corinthians 15:33). Just because others are cheating gives you no license to become a cheater yourself. If you find yourself surrounded by dishonesty, address it, and if that doesn't work, move on to protect your own reputation and soul.*
- *Your integrity sets an example: "In every way be an example of doing good deeds" (Titus 2:7). Show those around you that integrity is always the best policy!*
- *Integrity will be rewarded: "Because I am innocent, you support me and will let me be with you forever" (Psalm 41:12). You may not receive immediate rewards for your integrity, but you will be rewarded with a peaceful conscience for living right.*
- *The Lord hates lack of integrity: "Do not make plans to hurt your neighbors, and don't love false promises. I hate all these things" (Zechariah 8:16-17). Bottom line, we have been put on earth to praise and glorify God. If He hates—a very strong word—cheating, then we don't please Him when we practice it.*

The words you have said will be used to judge you. Some of your words will prove you right, but some of your words will prove you guilty.
Matthew 12:37

REAL LIFE

Worth More Than Gold

HUGH GILMORE

"I'm never going to make my end-of-quarter numbers," I groaned. "I was really counting on that bonus, too."

Dave just looked at me from across the table of the greasy spoon we frequented for lunch with a coy smile and a shake of his head.

"What?" I asked.

He shook his head again and then asked, "How long have you been with the company, man?"

"Two years. You know that."

"That explains things, then."

"Explains what?"

"How you make sure you get your bonus in a bad quarter. We've made our goals every month for the past two years, so you haven't learned how to work the system—yet."

He was right. Our company was growing by leaps and bounds with a couple of great new product lines, and if you were in sales, it was almost automatic that you'd hit your numbers every quarter. That's probably why I was counting on the bonus so much; I'd always received it like clockwork.

"What are you talking about?" I asked. "The system's pretty cut and dry. Hit your goals; get your bonus. Miss your goals; no bonus."

"Not so fast, my naïve young friend," Dave shot back. "It's simple. Are you good friends with any of your key account buyers?"

"Sure," I answered.

"Then get on the phone with them after we get back to work. Ask them to place a big order within the next three days. Then in a couple of weeks, when the dust settles and your bonus check is in hand, have them cancel the order. No one around here follows up on that stuff."

"I don't know, Dave."

"I usually send a nice little gift," he charged on, "like a new driver or an expensive bottle of Scotch, depending on the buyer, and everyone's happy."

My eyebrows were furrowed. I didn't say anything. Dave, who was suddenly uncomfortable due to my silence, kept shaking his head and looking anywhere else but at me.

On the way back to the office we were quiet for awhile before he said, "I'm not saying that what I just told you has actually happened. It probably has, though. At least I've heard rumors. You do what you want."

I wasn't going to say anything, but I finally blurted out, "I'm not going there, Dave. It's not worth getting caught. Plus, the company's been good to me. But the real reason is it's just not the right thing to do."

I was a little steamed as I finished.

"Like I said," Dave responded nonchalantly, "do what's right for you. Same as all of us. Probably doesn't even happen."

I missed my bonus—and lost a good friend in the process. We both gave our friendship the old college try, but we were now uncomfortable around each other. A few other guys shied away from me, too. I don't know what hurt most. But as tempted as I was, I didn't lose my integrity. And that's worth more than gold.

ACTION STEP

DO YOU HAVE A PERSONAL SET OF VALUES—THAT WILL GUIDE YOU WHEN YOU FEEL PRESSURED TO DO SOMETHING YOU'RE NOT SURE YOU WANT TO DO?

- BEGIN NOW TO WORK ON A PERSONAL VALUE STATEMENT THAT DECLARES WHAT CAN'T BE COMPROMISED IN YOUR LIFE.
- WHEN FINISHED, PUT IT ON AN INDEX CARD, HAVE IT LAMINATED, AND KEEP IT IN YOUR WALLET FOR EASY REFERENCE.

PRAYER

O God, You demand integrity because You are good and righteous—thank You for Your goodness. Lord, please continue to perfect my character and make my integrity rock solid.

GROWING STRONGER THROUGH ADVERSITY

WHEN FACED WITH SETBACKS AND OBSTACLES, GOD GIVES US THE GRACE TO ACCOMPLISH SPECTACULAR THINGS.

We shall draw from the heart of suffering itself the means of inspiration and survival.

WINSTON CHURCHILL

 TO THINK ABOUT

- What is the most difficult obstacle your have faced in your life?
- Who is someone you have seen overcome adversity? What was their secret?
- What can you do right now to prepare yourself to meet any challenge you face in life?

PROMISES

God will...

Be with you in difficulties
2 Chronicles 20:17

Make you more than a
conqueror
Romans 8:37

Produce perseverance
and character in you
Romans 5:3

Lead you in strength
Micah 2:13

Count It All Joy

BIBLE STUDY PASSAGE: ROMANS 8:10-39

My brothers and sisters, when you have many kinds of troubles, you should be full of joy, because you know that these troubles test your faith, and this will give you patience.   Let your patience show itself perfectly in what you do.   Then you will be perfect and complete and will have everything you need.

JAMES 1:2-4

No matter what our address, most of us live in a relatively healthy, secure, affluent society.   Such conditions make it easy to feel a sense of privilege, a sense that we deserve only good things in our lives—a peaceful and comfortable existence.

Innocent men and women all over the world know no such comfort.   In fact, living at the beginning of the third millennium since Christ's birth, there are more Christians martyred each year than in any previous decade of Christian history.

James, the brother of Jesus and the leader of the early church in Jerusalem, witnessed firsthand the horrors of persecution and hardship.

Yet he calls for his fellow believers to face all trials and tests with joy, faith, and optimism. He never asks for us to wish for hard times, but he does remind us that hard times—whether financial, physical, relational, or emotional—combined with faith, are opportunities for becoming a mature, spiritual person.

If you are facing adversity in your life right now, take heart, and know that God is doing something wonderful and new in your heart and life.

When you pass through the waters, I will be with you. When you cross rivers, you will not drown. When you walk through fire, you will not be burned, nor will the flames hurt you. This is because I, the Lord, am your God, the Holy One of Israel, your Savior. Isaiah 43:2-3

REAL LIFE

Paralyzed

KATHRYN LAY

Richard woke early that summer day, feeling achy.   He'd been laid off from his purchasing job two weeks before and I thought it was just stress.   But after taking a nap, he complained of numbness in his left cheek.

By afternoon, he couldn't close his left eye and the entire left side of his face was numb.   The word *stroke* exploded in my thoughts.

Our family doctor urged us to come in immediately.   Within an hour, we were given the news.

"It's not a stroke.   You have Bell's palsy."

Palsy.   Was it some type of disease that would spread through his body? The report was better than I feared—it would only affect his face.   He had an 80 percent chance of recovery.   But it could take a month, six months, or even a year.

Richard took the news with his usual optimism, but my throat ached at seeing him so uncomfortable.   The only pain he experienced was in his eye. Because he couldn't close it, there was no protection from wind and dirt, and it was beginning to dry out.   He had to wear a patch.

His efforts to smile often resembled a leer and, while we joked about it with friends, he felt hurt when strangers turned away.   Sometimes, people he dealt with treated him as if he were mentally impaired, speaking slowly and in simple words. I knew this hurt my college-educated husband with a teaching and business background.

The most discouraging problem Richard encountered was that of job interviews. His profession as a purchasing agent required a great deal of contact with buyers and sales people.   He was never offered a job during the time his face was paralyzed, though his résumé brought many interviews.

After learning he'd been turned down for another job, he said, "It's as if they believed my ability to do this job has been paralyzed. I'm sick of being rejected. There's nothing wrong with my mind."

I knew that. And so did God.

We were given anonymous gifts of food and money to pay bills, but Richard was frustrated at not working and providing for his family.

After two months of uncertainty, Richard noticed feeling and movement returning to his face. It wasn't long before he was almost back to normal. Less than a month after his recovery, he was hired for a job doing what he had done before.

My husband's paralysis was brief. Yet it taught him about God's faithfulness and provision. Richard remembered the fear and hurt at the way people treated him. But trusting in God's provision kept him going, and as always, God was beside us through all the hardships.

I may not be totally objective as his wife, but I believe Richard is a greater man today than he was before his paralysis.

ACTION STEP

WHAT IS THE HARSHEST SITUATION YOU ARE FACING IN YOUR LIFE RIGHT NOW? GIVE SERIOUS THOUGHT AND PRAYER TO THE QUESTION OF HOW GOD WANTS YOU TO GROW THROUGH THIS ADVERSITY. HOW CAN YOU WORK WITH GOD TO GROW, TO BECOME A MORE COMPLETE PERSON?

PRAYER

Lord, protect me and my loved ones from evil people, from disease, from temptations when faced with hardship. Please continue to make me who You want me to be.

OBEDIENCE

THOUGH IT'S SOMETIMES DIFFICULT,
WE PLEASE GOD AND LIVE THE LIFE
HE INTENDED FOR US WHEN WE
CHOOSE TO FAITHFULLY OBEY HIM.

One act of obedience is better
than one hundred sermons.

DIETRICH BOENHOEFFER

 To Think About

- Have you ever struggled with obedience because it seemed too hard and didn't make perfect sense?
- What are the benefits of obeying God?
- Is there an area of your life where you don't want to obey right now? What will you do about it?

PROMISES

God will...

Give you joy as
you trust Him
Psalm 33:21

Bless your obedience
Psalm 112:1

Take care of you as
you obey Him
Isaiah 1:19

Give you strength
Philippians 4:13

The Obedience of Mary

BIBLE STUDY PASSAGE: LUKE 1:26-56

Mary said, "I am the servant of the Lord.   Let this happen to me as you say!"

LUKE 1:38

Mary, the mother of Jesus, is perhaps the best known of all the women of the Bible—people across the world know who she was and honor her.   It was to Mary that God first revealed His specific plan to "save his people from their sins" through her Son (Matthew 1:21).

Mary was an ordinary young woman, engaged to a carpenter named Joseph, until one day, an angel suddenly appeared and said, "Greetings!   The Lord has blessed you and is with you" (Luke 1:28), changing her life forever.   The angel told her that she had been chosen to carry Jesus, the Savior of the world.

Mary could have asked a lot of questions—"What will Joseph think?"   "What will happen to us?"   If Mary was thinking these questions, she didn't say so.   She never argued or said, "Let me think this over."   She simply said yes to God's plan: "Let this happen to me as you say" (Luke 1:38). She placed her reputation, her marriage, and her entire life at risk to be obedient to God—and trusted that His will was perfect.

And because of her trust and obedience, salvation became available to all humanity.

Mary's simple faith and readiness to do God's will brought the blessing of God into her life—and that same faith and obedience will bless your life today.

Obey me, and I will be your God and you will be my people. Do all that I command so that good things will happen to you.

Jeremiah 7:23

REAL LIFE

Adoption

PAMELA WHITE

I met Kathy when I signed up for a year-long Bible study. We met once a week for what I thought would be a simple study course. It turned out to be so much more.

"Just do it," Kathy was told by a woman at a spiritual revival. Like the shoe commercial, that slogan became our spiritual battle cry.

The plight of Romanian orphanages had just become a matter of global importance, and one of Kathy's friends was gathering support to "adopt" an orphanage, even traveling to Romania to see the needs of the children firsthand. Kathy continually supported her friend and bought a sweatshirt with the shoe slogan, not knowing how much she would be challenged to "do" in the coming months.

Only later did she see the baby girl in a video brought back from Romania. In that moment, Kathy knew this child was to be her daughter.

Kathy asked for donated cribs, formula, and vitamins for the orphanage. Pray, she told us. Pray that people would be generous. Within four weeks she had 200 new cribs, several dozen cases of formula and vitamins, and cash donations to pay for some of the shipping. She called the president of the airline and asked him to transport the entire lot for free. He said no.

Pray, she told us. Pray that his heart would be softened. One week later, she asked again, and this time the answer was yes.

On the trip to deliver and set up the cribs, she spent time with the baby girl. Kathy's desire to adopt her was growing but so was the Romanian government's effort to slow down foreign adoptions.

Pray, she told us. Pray that the mayor of the village where the child was born would allow the adoption. We prayed.

We prayed. She began a search for someone who could translate for her. She found one Romanian restaurant listed in the yellow pages. The owner was willing to translate, especially when he found out the mayor they would be calling was his cousin!

We prayed on our knees for Kathy and her husband's safety during their next two trips to spend time with the girl while they worked to make the adoption happen. We prayed for the eighteen-month old girl who was the size of a six-month old and had never stood up.

We prayed without stopping as we collected formula, baby clothes, diapers, and more cribs for a second orphanage.

When they returned with their new tiny daughter, the child the entire church had already adopted in our hearts, there was cake, balloons, gifts for the family, and so many tears of joy. We sang and hugged, and promised to support this child in her Christian journey.

It was such a sweet day, such a beautiful reward for obeying God's call.

ACTION STEP

SECOND CHRONICLES 7:14 SAYS "THEN IF MY PEOPLE, WHO ARE CALLED BY MY NAME, ARE SORRY FOR WHAT THEY HAVE DONE, IF THEY PRAY AND OBEY ME AND STOP THEIR EVIL WAYS, I WILL HEAR THEM FROM HEAVEN. I WILL FORGIVE THEIR SIN, AND I WILL HEAL THEIR LAND."

WRITE OUT YOUR OWN PRAYER OF HUMBLE REPENTANCE, ASKING GOD TO FORGIVE AREAS OF DISOBEDIENCE AND HELP YOU MAKE ANY CHANGES IN YOUR LIFE THAT NEED TO BE MADE.

PRAYER

Father God, help me remember that Your will is good, pleasing, and perfect. I pray that Your will would be done in my life every day. Help me humbly follow You.

GOD DELIVERS

GOD HEARS THE PRAYERS OF THOSE WHO CALL TO HIM FOR MERCY.

*Those blessings that are sweetest are won
with prayers and worn with thanks.*

ANONYMOUS

TO THINK ABOUT

- Have you ever felt forgotten by God? Like He wasn't really working in your life?
- What situation are you praying about today?
- Why do you think we sometimes have to wait for God to accomplish something in our lives?

LESSON FOR LIFE

PROMISES

God will...

Protect you
Deuteronomy 33:29

Guide you
Isaiah 30:21

Use your trials for your
good
1 Peter 4:13

Never leave you
Hebrews 13:5

Hold On

BIBLE STUDY PASSAGE: GENESIS 50:15-26

You meant to hurt me, but God turned your evil into good
to save the lives of many people, which is being done.

GENESIS 50:20

God promised to make Abraham the father of a great nation, with descendants as numerous as the stars in the sky (Genesis 15:5). Despite his great faith, can you blame him for questioning when this was going to happen when he was still fatherless at age seventy-five (Genesis 12:4)?

Samuel anointed David as king of Israel in response to Saul's spirit of disobedience (1 Samuel 16:1). The problem was that David was hunted like a fugitive for the next seven years (1 Samuel 19:9). No wonder he cried to God, "Why have you forgotten me? Why am I sad and troubled by my enemies?" (Psalm 42:9).

Moses led the Hebrew slaves from captivity into the Promised Land—over the course of forty years (Exodus 16:35). Jesus spent the first thirty years of His life as a child, son, student, brother, and carpenter before the right moment came for Him to begin His ministry (Luke 3:23).

Why doesn't God just bring about His plans in our lives right now?   Could it be that one of the ways God makes us like Jesus is through allowing us to express our faith in Him through waiting?

In the Proverb, Solomon points out the natural truism that "Hope deferred makes the heart sick, but when the desire comes, it is a tree of life" (13:12 NKJV).   But Paul's testimony that "the sufferings we have now are nothing compared to the great glory that will be shown to us" (Romans 8:18) is a powerful reminder that God may not be early—but He's always right on time with just what we need.

Is your soul weary with worry?   Are you frustrated waiting to know God wants to do in your life?   Hold on.   God is on the way right now.

It is better to trust the Lord than to trust princes.
Psalm 118:9

REAL LIFE

One Day

C. HOPE FLINCHBAUGH

My little brother sat in my lap as Father told us the story. We all knew the story by heart, but it seemed more alive whenever Father told it.

"It was a miracle we made it out alive," he said. "The Muslims attacked our village with more machetes than there were people. Within minutes, the entire village was in flames and families—many of them from our church—were screaming and running in every direction."

Father paused, sucked in air and blew it out slowly. He always did that at this part.

"There was nothing to do but run. The next day, I buried the men who were killed."

"What happened to our cousins, Father?" I asked, leaning forward.

"All of the boys who were captured were forced to train in Sudan's government army. The girls—" Father looked at us with deep sadness in his eyes. "The girls were forced to become Muslim wives."

A cry for justice rose in my chest. How can I forgive such brutality?

When I think of Kenya, I remember the quiet, cool nights in the refugee camp. I often lay under the stars with the older guys and we talked about what it means to be Sudanese Christians. And we tried to forgive.

We planned to return to Sudan one day to rescue our Christian families and friends from their Muslim masters—a plan that never happened.

My keenest memory of the Kenyan refugee camp was hunger. Once a month the United Nations High Commission for Refugees dropped off a little rice or beans. I watched my mother hand each of us a plate of steaming rice, never lifting a spoon to her own mouth. Mother often ate one meal a month and the rest of the month she fasted and prayed that we would all leave Kenya one day. I was terrified she would die of hunger.

The happiest day of my life was when I trapped a bird underneath the round lid of a garbage can. I felt so proud when I watched Mother eat some of the stew she cooked from the bird I caught!

My faith in God soared the day I saw my mother waving papers.

"God has heard our prayers!" she shouted. "We're going to America!"

It was truly a miracle! Three things amazed me about the United States: food—piles of food in boxes, bags, cans, and freezers; snow—I'd never seen a snowflake or a snowball before; and freedom—I can pray without the fear of being beaten or kidnapped for exercising my faith.

In America, with a full stomach, it's easier to forgive the Sudanese soldiers. But I never forgot those dreams we talked about under the stars in Kenya. One day, after I get an American education, I want to go back to Sudan to help the people who were hurt by the Sudanese soldiers. I want to serve their daily needs, and then tell them the gospel.

ACTION STEP

SET UP A TIME TO SIT DOWN WITH AN OLDER ADULT WHO HAS WALKED WITH GOD A LONG TIME. ASK THEM TO SHARE A FEW STORIES ABOUT WHEN THEY HAD TO WAIT PATIENTLY FOR GOD TO ACT ON A SPECIAL NEED IN HIS OR HER LIFE.

PRAYER

Great is Your faithfulness, O God, my Redeemer.   Thank You for being true to Your word by never leaving or forsaking me.

TRUE SUCCESS

GOD MEASURES YOUR SUCCESS NOT JUST BY RESULTS BUT BY THE FAITHFULNESS OF YOUR SPIRIT.

*We never know, believe me,
when we have succeeded best.*

MIGUEL DE UNAMUNO

 To Think About

- 🗝 Have you ever given your best effort only to experience a great failure?
- 🗝 Conversely, have you ever experienced great success—even though you really didn't put your heart into something?
- 🗝 Is there something God wants you to work on right now?

LESSON FOR LIFE

PROMISES

God will...

Make great those who
serve
Matthew 20:26

Bless those who work
hard
Proverbs 22:29

Bless those who commit
their work to Him
Proverbs 16:3

Bless you
Psalm 84:11

A Faithful Heart

BIBLE STUDY PASSAGE:

The worries of this life, the temptation of wealth, and many other evil desires keep the teaching from growing and producing fruit in their lives.

MARK 4:19

Would you consider someone highly successful who was conceived out of wedlock? Who was born into a poor family? Who lost his father at an early age? Who was looked down on because of his race? Who was a simple manual laborer? Who was from a small town that was barely a dot on the map? Who depended on the gifts of others for food and shelter? Who was scorned by the religious and political leaders of his day? Who was arrested and imprisoned? Who was executed as a criminal?

Jesus, from an obscure country and city at the edge of the greatest kingdom in the world of its day, was all those things—and yet He changed the world. Jesus set aside all the trappings of worldly success in order to bring glory to His Heavenly Father (John 10:17).

He even warns His followers that loving Him may result in persecution (Matthew 10:17), loss of family (Matthew 10:21), and even death (Luke 21:16).

But He also assures us that there is no greater reward than doing the will of the Father in heaven (Matthew 16:27).

If you are discouraged with some of the results of your labor, remember that God spells success differently than the rest of the world. He spells it F-A-I-T-H-F-U-L-N-E-S-S.

There's nothing wrong with experiencing the kind of success that the world recognizes. Paul says, "In all the work you are doing, work the best you can" (Colossians 3:23). That will lead to accomplishments.

But if the choice before you is the applause of the world of the applause of heaven, only one reward is worth pursuing.

I, also, try to please everybody in every way. I am not trying to do what is good for me but what is good for most people so they can be saved.

1 Corinthians 10:33

REAL LIFE

Worth All the Money in the World

THERESE MARSZALEK

It arrived with little fanfare. My eyes locked on the envelope tumbling from the mountainous mail pile. Nestled inside was a report reflecting sales of my first book, along with my first royalty check. The anticipation was unbearable.

A couple of years earlier, the Lord prompted me to write a book, pouring the title, twelve chapter titles, and a vision of the cover into my heart.

He must have the wrong person, I thought. Reminding God of my shortcomings, I said, *But I've never written anything. I have no talent, no time, no experience.*

So, what did I have? He seemed to ask.

I had one thing: a desire to obey God.

I pressed through each step of the book, not realizing God was training me for future endeavors. Endless revisions brought much challenge. Although I accumulated enough reject letters to paper my office walls, doors began to open. As I remained committed to the process, God blessed my writing.

Two years later, I held the first copy of the book, an exact replica of the vision God had shown me. I had published over 100 magazine articles, secured a second publishing contract with a prominent Christian publisher, completed a third book, and was teaching writers' seminars.

What I thought was impossible, God made possible, doing immeasurably more than I asked or imagined. All He needed was a willing heart.

Tearing open the envelope, I froze. $35.99 flashed like a neon light. Knowing that most of the check resulted from books I had purchased, I calculated a net of $13.00, hardly enough to treat my family to a Big Mac.

"Well, hon," my husband joked. "I guess I'll have to wait to buy that new pickup truck."

Staring at the check, I felt as if I was being offered a platter of discouragement. Refusing the tempting offer, I roared with laughter. God reminded me of something I had almost forgotten. *Obedience and faithfulness is your part,* He said. *The results are up to Me.*

I sowed the royalty check, along with our tithe, into the Sunday offering. Although a small check, it represented more than anyone—anyone but God—could see.

A few months earlier, while I was enjoying breakfast with a group of women, a server asked, "How's your first book doing?"

"I don't know, Al," I said. "I haven't seen the first sales report."

Al wept, oblivious to the women's surprise at his sudden emotion. "Four of my friends committed their lives to Jesus while reading your book," he said. "And they're attending church too."

"Really?" I said, adding my own tears.

"I keep buying more copies to give away." Al wiped his wet cheeks. "I'm glad you obeyed God."

The next time I'm offered a platter of discouragement, I'll gladly say, "Thanks, but no thanks.   I'll pass." Obedience and faithfulness are my part. The results are up to God.

ACTION STEP

JESUS TELLS HIS DISCIPLES TO DO THEIR ACTS OF RIGHTEOUSNESS "IN SECRET" AND NOT FOR THE APPROVAL OF MEN (MATTHEW 6:4). WHAT IS ONE SMALL ONGOING TASK OF FAITHFULNESS YOU CAN TAKE ON THAT REMAINS STRICTLY BETWEEN YOU AND GOD ALONE—NOT EVEN FAMILY MEMBERS CAN KNOW!

THINK THROUGH HOW TO PULL THAT OFF AND LET IT BE A PRAYER OF FAITH TO YOUR HOLY FATHER.

PRAYER

Lord God, please make me more faithful to You. Please let my life be pleasing in Your sight.

RENEWAL

WE MUST KEEP OUR RELATIONSHIP WITH GOD FRESH AND NEW LEST WE LOSE THE JOY OF SALVATION.

Prayer is like the turning on of an electric switch.
It does not create the current; it simply provides a channel
through which the electric current may flow.

MAX HANDEL

TO THINK ABOUT

- How is your ardor toward God right now? Greater or less than it used to be?
- How do vibrant, joyful, enthused Christians lose their passion for God?
- Is it possible to always be "on fire" for God?

LESSON FOR LIFE

PROMISES

God will...

Comfort you
Psalm 119:50
Psalm 94:19

Give you a heart to
hear and obey Him
Ezekiel 36:26

Renew your heart
and mind
Hebrews 8:10

On the Mountaintop

BIBLE STUDY PASSAGE: JOHN 21:15-19

The teachings of the Lord are perfect; they give new strength.   The rules of the Lord can be trusted; they make plain people wise.

PSALM 19:7

Talk about the thrill of victory and the agony of defeat in one person's spiritual life!   Peter's journey with Jesus Christ was quite a roller coaster ride—

- *He was the first person to recognize Jesus as the Messiah—and cussed out a servant girl when she pointed out to the crowd that Peter was one of Jesus' followers (Matthew 16:16 and 26:71-74).*
- *He attacked a soldier, cutting off his ear, and was ready to fight to the death for Jesus—but he couldn't stay awake to pray with Him when Jesus really needed him, and he was nowhere to be found on the day of His crucifixion (John 18:10 and Matthew 26:40).*
- *He swore he would follow Jesus anywhere and everywhere no matter what the cost—but returned to fishing after the crucifixion (Luke 22:33 and John 21:3).*

234

But Peter didn't stay on the roller coaster. It was he who boldly preached to the crowds in Jerusalem even when authorities warned him not to (Acts 2:14); it was he who convinced the early Church that the gospel was for all people (Acts 10:34-45); and it was he who followed his Lord in death by crucifixion at the hands of the Romans.

Every relationship—including our relationship with God will have emotional highs and even lows. And though emotions are important, what matters most is faith—knowing and believing that God loves us and that we belong to Him.

If you are at a low ebb in your walk with Jesus, ask yourself—

- *Is there unconfessed sin in my life?*
- *Am I spending time each day in prayer and the Word?*
- *Am I following His plan and purpose for my life?*
- *Am I meeting regularly with others who love Jesus?*

Deal with whatever issues are unresolved, but then rest in the assurance of His love for you.

God, you are my God. I search for you. I thirst for you like someone in a dry, empty land where there is no water.
Psalm 63:1

 REAL LIFE

Holy Water

KAREN MAJORIS GARRISON

It hadn't rained for months. The parched, faded ground reminded me of myself. I walked along our fence, noticing the wilted flowers I had planted in the spring. Due to the drought, they had never thrived.

"Everything is dying, Lord," I whispered aloud.

Within two years my husband and I had lost several friends, then my mother-in-law, and soon after—my father-in-law. Although it had been nine months since my father-in-law's death, my heart ached. He'd been a vital part of our family. "It was only supposed to be routine surgery," I reminded the Lord, recalling the medical staff's errors. "And now he's gone."

I neared our porch, spotting the empty doghouse that awaited our dog's return. Even our beloved pet had been taken from us. One month after my father-in-law's failed surgery, Meshach, our black Labrador, had disappeared. *Where were You, Lord?* my heart cried. *Why didn't You keep those we love from harm? We trusted You!*

The previous year had sapped my strength, and like the earth beneath me, I felt withered. Even the Bible, which I routinely depended on to overcome obstacles, lay unopened on my nightstand for months.

Give me something, Father, I pleaded. *Anything to understand why You'd allow tragedies to those who have faith in You.*

And He did.

I remembered Job 13:15: "Though He slay me, yet I will trust Him."

Shaking my head, I wondered about the Lord's sense of humor. *Though He slay me, I will trust Him?* Was that verse supposed to make me feel better?

After heading into my house, I retrieved my Bible. My heart raced as I studied Job. Astounded at his declaration of trust after so much suffering, I read, re-read, and deliberated over the entire book. During that time, something happened inside of me. My spirit absorbed the power of God's Word, and my spiritual drought was ending.

The Book of Job never did answer my question of "why," but reminded me of "who" God is. No matter what, no matter what trials or tragedies, I must trust Him. In His ways, and not mine. I thought of my previous prayers concerning my loved ones. I had trusted that the Lord would answer my requests my way, not in His ways.

It had become night by the time I finished reading. I slipped outside to gaze at the stars and contemplate all that I'd read. As I lifted my head toward heaven, I felt raindrops.

Smiling, I lifted my hands in worship. My tears flowed, mixing with the rain's steady rhythm. Soaked, I stood there, absorbing what the Lord so freely gave.

And like the water, the holy water that descended from above to replenish the barren earth, God's Word had replenished my soul. They were one and the same—quenching, cleansing, and renewing.

Stepping back inside the house, I grinned, knowing that tomorrow my flowers would be standing tall—just like me.

ACTION STEP

ONE OF THE MOST BEAUTIFUL VERSES IN SCRIPTURE IS FOUND IN ISAIAH 40: "BUT THE PEOPLE WHO TRUST THE LORD WILL BECOME STRONG AGAIN. THEY WILL RISE UP AS AN EAGLE IN THE SKY; THEY WILL RUN AND NOT NEED REST; THEY WILL WALK AND NOT BECOME TIRED" (V. 31).

PULL AWAY FROM YOUR BUSY LIFE, TURN ON A PRAISE CD, AND LET GOD SPEAK TO YOUR HEART.

PRAYER

Father God, I never want to drift away from You—and yet I also know that I'm not always going to feel as close to You as I'd like to. Please give me courage to face the dry seasons in my faith with resolve, and joy in knowing You are always near.

ETERNAL LIFE

GOD'S GIFT OF SALVATION MEANS THAT WE WILL LIVE FOREVER IN GLORY.

Earth has no sorrow that Heaven cannot heal.

SIR THOMAS MOORE

TO THINK ABOUT

- Why is there so little talk about heaven?
- Why is heaven so hard to describe?
- What are some of the images that flash in your mind when you think of heaven?

PROMISES

God will...

Prepare something
wonderful for those who
love Him
1 Corinthians 2:9

Save those who believe
in Him
John 3:16

Heal in heaven
Revelation 21:4

Prepare a place without
pain or darkness
Revelation 22:5

The Glory of Heaven

*There are many rooms in my Father's house; I would not
tell you this if it were not true. I am going there to
prepare a place for you.*

JOHN 14:2

Paul wrote this to a group of Christians who were experiencing intense persecution: "The sufferings we have now are nothing compared to the great glory that will be shown to us" (Romans 8:18).

While it's true that our focus needs to be on serving God and others today (Matthew 6:33); and while it's also true that we can experience the full riches of heaven right now (Ephesians 2:6); it is also true that we receive comfort and encouragement as we think about our future in heaven.

Heaven truly is a wonderful place!

- *It's a place of beauty: "No one has ever seen this, and no one has ever heard about it. No one has ever imagined what God has prepared for those who love him" (1 Corinthians 2:9). No words can adequately describe the wonder of heaven.*

240

- *It's a place of restoration: "He will wipe away every tear from their eyes, and there will be no more death, sadness, crying, or pain, because all the old ways are gone" (Revelation 21:4). All sorrows and infirmities disappear and are healed in heaven.*
- *It's a place of divine presence: "Now God's presence is with people, and he will live with them, and they will be his people. God himself will be with them and will be their God" (Revelation 21:3). We know Jesus and love Jesus right now. But think how wonderful it will be to see Him face-to-face.*
- *It's a place of purity: "There will never be night again. They will not need the light of a lamp or the light of the sun, because the Lord God will give them light" (Revelation 22:5). Sin and anything that distorts the true pleasures and fulfillment of humanity will no longer corrupt.*
- *It's a place of joy "Because you were loyal with small things, I will let you care for much greater things. Come and share my joy with me" (Matthew 25:21). Think of the happiest day you have ever experienced. It will not compare to the joy you will celebrate in heaven.*

A final benefit of thinking about heaven is that it motivates us to serve God joyfully now—and reach out to family, friends, and even enemies with the love of God.

We know that our body—the tent we live in here on earth—will be destroyed. But when that happens, God will have a house for us. It will not be a house made by human hands; instead, it will be a home in heaven that will last forever.

2 Corinthians 5:1

 REAL LIFE

Our Mansion

MELVA COOPER

My six year-old granddaughter, Mary Kathryn, and I had one of our famed "girls' days." She loves for me to pick her up after school and take her to the dollar store. There she chooses a few things to buy just for herself.

When we returned home, Mary Kathryn began playing with her new things she had gotten for her Barbies. I soon discovered she was pondering deeply while carefully arranging the Barbies in their new room she had just purchased.

She startled me with these words, "Grandma, I have a mansion in heaven!"

Excitedly, I replied that I sure hoped my mansion was next to hers. Mary Kathryn casually continued the conversation with, "My mother's will be on the other side."

And then without thinking any further she uttered ever so longingly, "I really want Blake's mansion to be right in back of mine." Immediately, I knew she was speaking about her twelve-year-old friend who drowned earlier that summer. They had played together all of her life. Mary Kathryn joyfully antici-pates going to heaven where she can resume her friendship with Blake.

I do not have all the answers about mansions in heaven. I do know I can look forward to everlasting life because Jesus has promised it to all who believe in Him.

Mary Kathryn's young understanding was visualizing all those mansions adjacent to one another. I thanked God for giving Mary Kathryn a concept of heaven at such a tender age.

I also thanked God that my dear granddaughter had received Jesus Christ as her personal Savior a few months earlier—which meant that she not only knew about heaven, she also knew without a doubt that she would live there with God—and her friend Blake—forever.

Make those mansions close to Your heavenly throne where we will be praising and worshipping You forever, became my prayer.

ACTION STEP

WHO WILL BE IN HEAVEN BECAUSE OF YOU? THE SONG BY RAY BOLTZ SAYS, "THANK YOU FOR GIVING TO THE LORD. I AM A LIFE THAT WAS CHANGED."

WRITE DOWN FIVE NAMES OF THOSE WHO NEED TO KNOW GOD. BEGIN PRAYING FOR THEIR SOUL TODAY. ASK GOD TO HELP YOU REACH OUT TO THEM AT THE RIGHT TIME IN THE RIGHT PLACE.

PRAYER

Father God, thank You so much that You have provided a place without pain and a way to get there. Please help me today to reflect the glory of heaven in my life right now.

A PRAYER FOR YOUR SOUL

The most important soul matter, of course, is having a relationship with God. Everything in our lives—everything in our entire existence—has new, eternal meaning when we understand that God loves us and has made a way to save us through Jesus Christ. All of this may be new to you. If you'd like to know that you have a lasting relationship with God through Jesus, pray this prayer:

Heavenly Father, I come to You admitting that I am a sinner. I believe that Your Son, Jesus, died on the cross and rose from the dead to take away my sins. Jesus, I choose to follow You and ask that You fill me with the Holy Spirit so that I can understand more about You. Thank You for adopting me, and thank You that I am now a child of God. Amen.

HOW TO READ AND STUDY THE BIBLE

One of the most important keys to nurturing your soul is consistent reading and studying of Scripture. If you're a new Bible reader, be patient with yourself! Learn to study and apply God's Word one step at a time.

1. **Have your own Bible.** *Your own Bible is the one that has your name in it, the one that you not only carry to church, but even remember to bring home with you. You need a Bible that you cherish and keep close at hand.*

2. **Begin with prayer.** *Every time you sit down to read your Bible, ask God to speak to you through Scripture. Let Him know you are ready and willing to hear His voice.*

3. **Plan a Bible-reading schedule.** *You will profit more from Bible reading if you study entire books at a time, not just parts here and there. So map out a good Bible-reading schedule, planning which books to work through several at a time.*

4. **Use a study method.** *Discipline in Bible study is just like discipline in any other area—discipline leads to positive and healthy experiences in our lives.*

If you keep a notebook or prayer journal, you might start a section titled "My Time in the Word." As you learn one simple Bible study method, you'll see how a notebook can be used to make your time in the Word more effective.

Step One:

LOOK FOR THE BIG PICTURE

Before focusing on several verses of a particular chapter, get an overall idea of the book you are reading. Try to find out who is writing the book, to whom, and why. Many Bibles contain a short introduction to each book of the Bible with a lot of this information given. Another way to do this is to read the entire book quickly; if it is a longer book, simply skim through it and note the paragraph headings printed in your Bible. You're not trying to read every word, just get acquainted with the flow and feeling of the book.

Step Two:

SELECT A STUDY PASSAGE

Once you have an idea of the big picture, you'll want to study the entire book in chunks—anywhere from a few verses to an entire chapter at a time.

When you study a passage, what counts is quality of reading, not quantity. One caution: You will not want to break up paragraphs, or you will lose the writer's train of thought.

Step Three:

READ THE STUDY PASSAGE SEVERAL TIMES

After you choose the verses you are going to study, read that section of scripture at least two times. Three or four times would be better. And remember, you set the pace—you can choose to study a chapter or just a few verses. What counts is that you grow in an understanding of God's Word.

Step Four:

SEARCH FOR MAJOR TRUTHS

As you read through your study passage for the third or fourth time, note the key thoughts found there. What does the writer want the people who read this to understand? Look for commands to be obeyed, warnings to be heeded, promises to be claimed, and truths to be believed.

Set aside a space in your journal for you to jot down these key thoughts and major truths.

Step Five:

ASK QUESTIONS

Now is the time to raise questions that come to your mind. Not everything in Scripture is immediately or easily understood. Do not be surprised or intimidated by this fact.

Write down your questions in your notebook or journal. Here are several places where you can go to get answers to these questions.

• **Scripture:** Use a concordance or study Bible to look up passages of scripture that deal with the subject you're studying—often, one scripture can help explain another.

• **Commentaries:** Commentaries study and explain Bible passages a little at a time. Your church library probably contains several sets of commentaries you could borrow.

• **Pastors and teachers:** Your pastor and Sunday school teachers may not be able to give you an answer right away, but they will be willing to search for answers with you.

Step Six:

PUTTING IT INTO PRACTICE

You need to apply the Bible to your life now. "Do not merely listen to the word ... Do what it says" (1:22) was James' advice.

Is there something you are doing that you shouldn't be doing? Is there something you are not doing that you need to be doing? Is there something about God or Jesus or the Holy Spirit that you did not know before? Do you need to be more sensitive to someone at work? Do you need to seek someone's forgiveness? Do you need to forgive someone?

Step Seven:

NOTE A VERSE TO REMEMBER

The final step in your Bible study is to take one last look at your study passage and write down a verse or two that you want to remember most. Memorizing scripture is a terrific discipline. It allows you to take scripture with you, even when you don't or can't have your Bible at hand.

Writing out a key verse will make remembering it much easier for you. It is a good start to memorizing it also.

May God cause your soul to stretch and grow
as you embark on a journey through His Word!

Acknowledgements

"A Feast of Faith" © Stan Toler From *God Is Never Late; He's Seldom Early; He's Always Right on Time*, published 2004. Used by permission of Beacon Hill Press.

"The Bible that Wouldn't Go Away" © Lena Hunt Mabra. Used by permission. All rights reserved

"A Note of Thanks" © Max Davis. Used by permission. All rights reserved.

"Poinsettias in Bloom" © Nanette Thorsen-Snipes. Used by permission. All rights reserved.

"Faith, Not Fear" © Brenda Nixon. Used by permission. All rights reserved.

"Gustel's Tulips" © Pat Butler. Used by permission. All rights reserved.

"New Heart, New Eyes" © Lee Warren. Used by permission. All rights reserved.

"The Least of These" © Nanette Thorsen-Snipes. Used by permission. All rights reserved.

"Death and Life..." © Max Davis. Used by permission. All rights reserved

"My Little Wooden Cup" © Glenda Palmer. Used by permission. All rights reserved.

"Just a Little Lie" © Jennifer Johnson. Used by permission. All rights reserved.

"A Real Bear" © Mark Gilroy Communications. Used by permission. All rights reserved.

"Just Like My Daddy" © Linda Rondeau. Used by permission. All rights reserved.

"No More Tears" © Joan Clayton. Used by permission. All rights reserved.

"When God Says No" © Paula L. Silici. Used by permission. All rights reserved.

"The Question that Changed My Life" © Kitty Chappell. Used by permission. All rights reserved.

"Sweet Surrender" © Therese Marszalek. Used by permission. All rights reserved.

"Sabbath Rest" © Jan Wilson. Used by permission. All rights reserved.

"A Special Christmas Story" © Joanne Schulte. Used by permission. All rights reserved.

"Drained by Debt" © Eileen Key. Used by permission. All rights reserved.

Your Story

Has there been a time in your life when you encountered God in a powerful way that changed and enriched your soul? Would your story encourage others to grow closer to God and improve their lives?

WE WOULD LOVE TO CONSIDER YOUR STORY FOR FUTURE EDITIONS OF SOUL MATTERS. PLEASE SHARE YOUR STORY TODAY, WON'T YOU? FOR WRITER'S GUIDELINES, UPCOMING TITLES, AND SUBMISSION PROCEDURES, VISIT:

www.soulmattersbooks.com

Or send a postage-paid, self-addressed envelope to:

**Mark Gilroy Communications, Inc.
6528 E. 101st Street, Suite 416
Tulsa, Oklahoma 74133-6754**